# Communication in the Classroom
## Applications and Methods
## for a Communicative Approach

**Longman Handbooks for Language Teachers**
General Editor: Donn Byrne

The Teaching of Literature – H L B Moody
The Teaching of Pronunciation – Brita Haycraft
The Language Laboratory and Language Learning – Julian Dakin
Writing English Language Tests – J B Heaton
Visual Materials for the Language Teacher – Andrew Wright
Teaching Oral English – Donn Byrne
Selections from 'Modern English Teacher' – edited by Helen Moorwood
An Introduction to English Language Teaching – John Haycraft
Teaching Writing Skills – Donn Byrne
Drama in Language Teaching – Susan Holden
Communication in the Classroom – edited by Keith Johnson and Keith
  Morrow

Longman Handbooks for Language Teachers
General Editor: Donn Byrne

# Communication in the Classroom
## Applications and Methods for a Communicative Approach

**Edited by Keith Johnson**
Centre for Applied Language Studies, University of Reading

**and Keith Morrow**
Bell Educational Trust

**Longman**

LONGMAN GROUP LIMITED
Longman House,
Burnt Mill, Harlow, Essex

*Associated companies, branches and representatives
throughout the world*

© Longman Group Ltd. 1981

First published 1981

ISBN 0 582 74605 1

Printed in Great Britain by
Spottiswoode Ballantyne Ltd.,
Colchester and London.

**for Kate and Tanya**

# Preface

Recent years have seen many exciting developments in language teaching. Some have been at the level of syllabus design and are associated with the concepts of 'notional' and 'functional' syllabuses. Others are concerned with methodology and we are today seeing the growth of interesting new procedures and techniques, many of which challenge our traditional views of what should happen in the classroom.

It is true that these various developments relate to different stages in the teaching operation; it is also true that they have not yet come together to produce what can justifiably be called a coherent new approach to language teaching. Yet there does exist behind them a common set of assumptions, and it is the existence of this shared background which gives us the justification for referring to the new developments under the single label of 'communicative language teaching'.

Many articles and books have already been written on the subject of communicative language teaching. But most have been theoretical in nature and may well leave the practising language teacher wondering how the new ideas can actually be applied to the classroom. The aim of this volume is to answer precisely this question. The contributors have been chosen because of their practical experience as materials producers or teachers. They have written for the classroom teacher in an attempt to point out some of the implications – and some of the problems – associated with 'being communicative' in the classroom. The book will also be useful for trainee teachers or those following in-service training courses – in fact for anyone interested in knowing what communicative language teaching means in practical terms.

The book is divided into two main parts, preceded by an introductory paper which sketches some of the background to communicative language teaching and attempts definitions of crucial terms (like 'notional' and 'functional', as well as the term 'communicative' itself).

Part A deals primarily (though not exclusively) with syllabus and course design, and nearly all of its contributors have had direct experience in the production of communicatively-orientated materials. One of the aims of this Part is purely descriptive – we wanted the contributors to describe how they faced the problems posed by the production of communicative materials for various types of student. But the Part also contains an element of polemic. It was not our intention here to provide a unified view – on the contrary we wanted to provide a series of 'forum sections' reflecting a variety of approaches and opinions relating to questions of course design. Thus although there are considerable areas of agreement among the contributors, there are also differences and one of the aims of this Part was to draw attention to these.

There are certain groups of students for which the application of a communicative approach poses particular problems. Among these are the various types of beginner (adult, primary and 'false'), and the 'general', non-ESP student whose communicative needs may be difficult to specify. It is on these 'problematic' areas that Part A concentrates: Section One on adult beginners; Section Two on primary and false beginners; Section Three on the 'general' student.

Part B is mainly concerned with methodology. The introductory paper sets the scene by attempting to draw together some of the strands that might make up a communicative methodology. As this paper makes clear, we are not yet at the point where we may speak of an overall and coherent method. However, it establishes five principles which might stimulate thought in this direction.

The remaining papers are divided into two sections. Section One re-examines the traditional 'four skills' from a communicative point of view and considers some of the implications of this re-appraisal. Section Two is the most directly practical of the book. It looks at the classroom possibilities offered by a variety of communicatively-orientated activities.

All the papers in this volume have been specially written, and none has yet appeared elsewhere. We felt it necessary to commission papers in this way to provide the kind of coverage of the subject which we thought the practising teacher would want. We hope that this has resulted in a book which, while expressing many different standpoints, provides a coherent overview of what a communicative approach to language teaching might involve.

KJ
KM
January 1980

# Contents

# Introduction

## KEITH JOHNSON    Some background, some key terms and some definitions

### 1 Introduction

This book is about communicative language teaching, and in its pages (as in the pages of many books and articles written nowadays) certain key terms recur time and time again. Predominant among these are 'notion(al)', 'function(al)', 'communicative' and 'syllabus'. In fact, the use of the first three of these terms is by now so widespread that they are often used – quite wrongly – as synonyms. Because of the importance of these terms and the frequent confusion in their use, it seems appropriate that the first paper in this collection should attempt to provide definitions. At the same time the paper will sketch, in broad outline, the background essential to an understanding of the current trends in language teaching which are the subject of this book.

### 2 Some background

In language teaching, as in other fields, new movements often begin as reactions to old ones. Their origins, that is, lie in a discontent with an existing state of affairs. We might begin our consideration of communicative language teaching, therefore, by looking at the discontent which teachers and applied linguists in the 1960s felt towards the kind of language teaching then predominant. This discontent is vividly expressed by Newmark (1966) who speaks of the 'structurally competent' student – the one, that is, who has developed the ability to produce grammatically correct sentences – yet who is unable to perform a simple communicative task. His example of such a task is 'asking for a light from a stranger'. Our structurally competent student might perform this task in a perfectly grammatical way by saying 'have you fire?' or 'do you have illumination?' or 'are you a match's owner?' (Newmark's examples). Yet none of these ways – however grammatical they may be – would be used by the native speaker.

Most of us are familiar with this phenomenon of the structurally competent but communicatively incompetent student, and he bears striking witness to the truth of the one insight which, perhaps more than any other, has shaped recent trends in language teaching. This is the insight

1

that ability to manipulate the structures of the language correctly is only a part of what is involved in learning a language. There is a 'something else' that needs to be learned, and this 'something else' involves the ability to be appropriate, to know the right thing to say at the right time. 'There are', in Hymes's (1970) words, 'rules of use without which the rules of grammar would be useless'.

It is not difficult to see how this phenomenon of the structurally competent but grammatically incompetent student came about. It is to a large extent the result of the kind of language teaching which, influenced heavily by the audio-lingual tradition, places strong emphasis on what Newmark and Reibel (1968) call 'mastery of language structure'. In this kind of language teaching the predominant (though it would be an exaggeration to say exclusive) emphasis is on teaching the students how to 'form' correctly; how, that is, to manipulate the structures of the language easily and without error. The result of this emphasis has been – in the best of cases – students who know their grammar but lack the 'something else'.

The emphasis on mastery of structure manifested itself at every stage of the teaching operation, not least at the stage of syllabus design. A syllabus is in general terms a 'list of items we wish to teach', and if we see our main aim as being the teaching of structures then it is entirely natural that our syllabuses, as 'lists of items to teach', should be lists of structures. This is more or less what, until recent times, syllabuses have been.

How can the situation be changed? How, in other words, can we provide the student with the 'something else' essential to communicative ability? We can approach one possible answer to these questions by returning to Newmark's example of the student who does not know how to ask for a light from a stranger. It may well be, we could argue, that the student is unable to perform this communicative task simply because we have never considered items like 'asking for a light from a stranger' (or, in more general terms, 'requesting services') as part of our teaching content. Once, we might say, we are prepared to accept that we have actually to give lessons teaching things like 'requesting services', the battle will be half won.

The implications in this line of argument for syllabus design are clear. If a syllabus is a 'list of items we wish to teach' and if we are prepared to see language learning as a question of mastering not only structures but also 'meanings' or 'uses', then our syllabuses must list items of 'meaning' or 'use' as well as items of structure. Suddenly the traditional view of the syllabus as a list of structures becomes inadequate.

But how do you list 'meanings' or 'uses'? This is one of the problems which a team of experts convened by the Council of Europe in 1971 set out to answer. The brief of this team was to work towards the development of a language teaching system suitable for teaching all the languages used in the Council's member countries. One member of that team, D A Wilkins, had the particular task of developing a system of categories by means of which it would be possible to specify the communicative needs of the adult learner working within a European context. It is at this point that 'notions' and 'functions' enter the scene.

## 3 Notions and functions: definitions

In 1972, as part of the Council of Europe's work, Wilkins wrote a paper proposing that two categories of 'meaning' and 'use' might be suitable for the purposes of syllabus design. The first category he calls 'semantico-grammatical' and this is composed of items akin to what in everyday speech we call 'concepts'. Examples of these categories, taken from Wilkins's list are: *frequency*, *duration*, *location* and *quantity*. They are 'semantic' categories because they are items of meaning. But Wilkins includes the word 'grammatical' in his label to recognise the fact that, in most European languages at least, these categories relate fairly directly to grammatical categories. Consider, for example, how we express the concept of *frequency* in English. There are a fairly restricted set of grammatical means for doing this involving, among other things, choice of tense (the simple tenses usually being used to express habitual action), and certain frequency adverbials.

Wilkins's second category is the 'communicative function'. Communicative functions are, in broad terms, the *uses* to which we put language. Examples taken from his paper are: *requesting information, expressing disapproval, greeting* and *inviting*. His list also includes *requesting services,* under which Newmark's 'asking for a light from a stranger' might fall. These categories of communicative function have come to be known, for the sake of brevity, as 'functions'. They do not, unlike the semantico-grammatical categories, relate directly to grammatical categories. Thus if we consider a function like *inviting* we find various, quite grammatically distinct ways of performing the function. Examples might be 'would you like to + INF', 'how about + ING', 'why not + INF', 'do + IMPERATIVE'.

Wilkins's proposal is, then, that we should use his semantico-grammatical and functional categories as the means of listing concepts and uses in our syllabus. He uses the term 'notional syllabus' (the title of his 1976 book) to describe a syllabus containing such lists. In this phrase he is using the word 'notional' as an umbrella term to refer to his two categories, thereby expressing the fact that they are indeed categories of meaning (though as we have seen, the semantico-grammatical categories do relate significantly to structural categories). This terminology suggests the diagram on the next page:

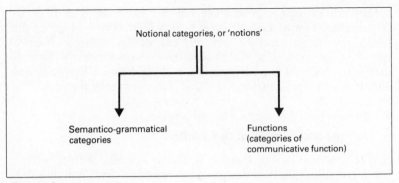

*Figure 1*

Whereas the term 'categories of communicative function' can be succinctly abbreviated to 'functions', no similar abbreviation is unfortunately readily available for the term 'semantico-grammatical categories'. It may be that this simple and banal fact is responsible for the considerable confusion that has grown up over the use of the word 'notional'. For it is as an abbreviation for 'semantico-grammatical category' that the word 'notion' has come to be used. Van Ek (1975) uses the word in this way, and it is a usage that can be justified. If 'concept' is a rough synonym for Wilkins's 'semantico-grammatical category', then is not 'notion' a rough synonym for 'concept'? This second terminology can be expressed by the following diagram:

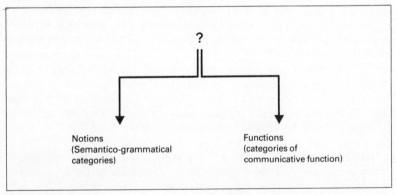

*Figure 2*

Figures 1 and 2 show the ambiguity with which the terms 'notion' and 'notional syllabus' are used. In the first terminology a 'notional syllabus' would be one which listed functional as well as semantico-grammatical categories; in the second terminology it would be one which listed semantico-grammatical categories only.

Figure 2 lacks an umbrella term. The aim of this paper is to record how terms *are* used, not to suggest how they *should be* used. But perhaps an umbrella term like 'semantic categories' would be appropriate. We could then use 'notion' as in Figure 2, and could speak of 'semantic syllabuses' and 'notional syllabuses' without fear of ambiguity. This terminology will be followed for the rest of this paper.[1]

## 4 Notions and functions: the difference

The question is sometimes asked: what is the difference between a notion and a function? The distinction is certainly a difficult one to express in precise terms, and the use of rather vague words like 'concepts' and 'uses' to distinguish the two often simply leads to further confusion. For if we say that a function is a 'use to which we put language', we are open to the response that *expressing frequency* (*frequency* being one of Wilkins's semantico-grammatical categories) is a 'use to which we put language'. Similarly it is difficult to define a sense in which *frequency* can be said to be a concept, while *sympathy* (a function in Wilkins) is not.

A full answer to the question would be concerned with levels of analysis. Just as grammatical analysis operates on different levels – the morpheme, the phrase, the clause etc – so too must the analysis of 'meaning'. Indeed, we do not have to go far into the analysis of extended stretches of language to realise that the two terms 'notion' and 'function' are paltry tools for analysis and need considerable enrichment.[2] But the question of levels of analysis would take us far beyond our immediate concerns, and as a loose rule of thumb we might say that we can identify the *function* of a spoken utterance by asking the question: 'what was the speaker's intention in saying it?'. The answer, depending on the utterance and its context, might be 'to greet', 'to invite', 'to express sympathy'; these, we would say, are the utterances' functions.

Once we become accustomed to asking this question about speaker intention we soon find that the same 'sentence' can function in different ways, according to context. Take, for example, the sentence 'you will come tomorrow' said by a father to his child. This may be intended to function as a *command* – meaning roughly 'you just make sure you come tomorrow'. It might, on the other hand, be intended as a *promise*, paraphrased by 'Don't worry. Whatever happens I'll make sure you're allowed to come tomorrow'. We would probably need information about the utterance's context before being able to decide its function.

We can analyse the same sentence – 'you will come tomorrow' – at a different level, to discover what 'concepts' or 'notions' it conveys. One such concept is that of 'a person present, other than the speaker', conveyed by the word 'you'. There is also the concept of futurity, expressed by the use of 'will'. Notice that a 'notional' analysis of this kind will *not* reveal the speaker's intention (and hence the utterance's function). An analysis of the concepts expressed in a sentence will not tell us why that sentence was said.

The above discussion may reveal one important point about 'notional' and 'functional' analysis – that sentences express *both* notions *and* functions. So the question 'does this sentence express notions or functions?' is a meaningless one. It is like asking whether a sentence contains words or clauses or whether a car has wheels or brakes!

## 5 The analysis of language needs

Wilkins's work provides a framework for listing 'meanings' for the purposes of syllabus design. The next problem which the Council of Europe team faced was how to decide *which meanings* to teach. The problem is to a large extent a new one for syllabus designers and to understand in what sense it is new, consider the process by which traditional 'structural' syllabuses are developed. The structural syllabus designer would know what grammar points his students had already learned, and he would select from the remainder of the structures of the language those which he felt his students should acquire next. This selection would constitute his syllabus.

In this process the designer's ultimate aim is clear – to teach all the structures of the language, working through them in 'graded' fashion. But the situation becomes more complex when we deal with categories of meaning. Consider functions for example (though what is said below could apply equally well to notions). It is clear that the uses to which a language may be put are very many; we cannot teach all the functions of English in the same way we might teach all the structures. Some criterion of selection is needed which will identify those functions which a particular group of students will find especially useful. Once identified, these can be taught to the exclusion of other, less necessary, ones.

How can the particularly useful functions (and notions) be identified? The Council of Europe team, particularly Richterich (1973), attempted to do this by looking closely at the 'language needs' of groups of learners. Language needs are, in Richterich's (1973) words, 'the requirements which arise from the use of language in the multitude of situations which may arise in the social lives of individuals and groups'. A key word in this quotation is 'situation'. It is by looking at the situations in which our students will want to use English that we shall be able to decide which functions and notions (and which language forms associated with each) it will be most useful to teach.

But what is a 'situation'? One dictionary[3] defines it as a 'set of circumstances' and van Ek (thinking of situations specifically in relation to language use) talks of 'the complex of extra linguistic conditions which determines the nature of the language-act' (1973). The words 'set' and 'complex' are important here because they convey the idea that the factors which go to make up a situation (and hence 'determine the nature of the language-act') are numerous. What exactly these factors are cannot be considered here, but three central ones may be mentioned in passing. These are *setting* (where the speakers are – at the airport, in a shop etc); *role* (what the relationship between the speakers is – friend/ friend, customer/shop assistant etc) and *topic* (what the speakers are talking about – pastimes, business etc).

The process of analysing language needs which has here been outlined is, then, one which begins with the question 'in what situations will my students want to use English?' It looks at the various factors involved in the concept of situation, identifies important notions/ functions and the language forms associated with each. It is a process which is nowadays widespread and various models based on this general paradigm have been developed. Predominant among these is Munby's (1978) model. The obvious advantage of this approach is that it enables us to develop syllabuses sensitive to the needs of different groups of learners. But this advantage brings with it a problem. In the case of an ESP group (a group of secretaries or lawyers for example) the identification of a common set of language needs is a feasible proposition. But what about the 'general' group which contains lawyers, secretaries, doctors, mechanics, and a selection of students who are learning English for rather vague purposes – 'just to talk to people', for example, though they may not be sure exactly to whom? And what about children, whose eventual needs for English (if indeed they are to have any) cannot be predicted – and even if they could would almost certainly differ from pupil to pupil?

Part A of this book contains articles by contributors who have struggled with these problems and who offer suggestions for solving them. But one particular solution, the Council of Europe's, may be mentioned here. Their team encountered the problem in an extreme form since their brief was to develop a framework for the most general and vague of audiences – the average adult European, living in any of a number of countries, wishing to learn any of a number of languages for any of a number of purposes. The chief prerequisite for such a framework is clearly flexibility and for this reason the team developed what they call a 'unit/credit' system. In this system areas of language use are divided into 'units'. Since different areas of use will be relevant to the needs of different groups of learners, students are guided as to which units to cover. Credits are given for units completed and when a number of credits have been gained, a qualification is given.

The aspect of this system most relevant to the present discussion is the concept of the 'common core'. The team recognised that there will be areas of interest common to all students whatever their situations and specialisations. There will be a common core of functions (for example) relevant to secretary as much as engineer, doctor as much as mechanic.

Each learning level in the Council of Europe's system will thus have a common core of units alongside those specialised ones which students select according to needs. Much of the above discussion has concerned the Council of Europe's work. In a paper discussing the aims of this team, Trim (1973) notes that it is 'common practice' to recognise five levels of language proficiency, the lowest of which he calls *The Threshold Level*. One member of the team, van Ek, was given the task of providing a syllabus specification for this level. This appears in two forms – van Ek (1975) for the adult learner and van Ek (1978) for the secondary school student. Initially *The Threshold Level* was conceived of as 'a minimum level of foreign language competence ... below which no further levels can be usefully distinguished' (van Ek, 1973). Later, however, a specification for a level below *Threshold* was considered necessary. This specification was produced under the title of *Waystage* (van Ek and Alexander, 1977).

## 6 Syllabus inventories and syllabuses

Before beginning any teaching operation we list the items we wish our students to learn. If our syllabus is structural we might as a first stage list the grammatical items under such headings as 'verb constructions', 'noun phrase constructions' and so on. This initial list would not be ordered for teaching purposes. Thus the fact that 'verb constructions' might appear on our list before 'noun phrase constructions' would not imply that we teach the former before the latter. The essential job of grading and combining the structures into sequences for teaching would constitute the second stage of our operation. Only when this has been done can we say that we have a fully-fledged syllabus. We might distinguish the initial unordered list from the final ordered one by calling the former a 'syllabus inventory' and the latter a 'syllabus'.[4] The distinction applies as much to semantic syllabus design as to structural syllabus design and according to this terminology specifications like *The Threshold Level* are syllabus inventories. As it happens, van Ek (1975) lists notions before functions; as it also happens, the function of *narrating* is listed before the function of *greeting*. This ordering is about as significant as the order of names in a telephone directory; the implication is neither that notions should be taught before functions, nor *narrating* before *greeting*.

But when we consider semantic as opposed to structural syllabus design one further step is required to convert a syllabus inventory into a syllabus. This is because semantic syllabus inventories contain not one, but many lists – not just structures but notions, functions, settings, topics, roles (and often other types of category) as well. We clearly cannot devise a programme to teach language associated with each of these lists in turn – for example covering notions in Year 1, functions in

Year 2, settings in Year 3 and so on. We must select one of these types of item as our 'unit of organisation'. We might for example decide that each teaching unit of our course should cover one function. The result would be, in the terminology used in this paper, a 'functional syllabus' Such a syllabus would of course not *ignore* the other types of list on the inventory. We would have to ensure that the language presented under the various functional headings took account of the settings, topics, notions etc on our inventory. But we will have selected the function as our 'unit of organisation' for the syllabus.

The question of 'unit of organisation' is important for two reasons. Firstly it leads us to realise that a *syllabus inventory* of the *Threshold Level* type can lead to *syllabuses* of different orientations. Thus instead of selecting the function as our unit of organisation we might equally well have chosen the notion (with lessons on *frequency, location* etc), the setting (at the airport, in a shop etc), the topic (pastimes, education etc) and so on. The result would then be notional, setting-based or topic-based syllabuses. The question of how we decide which type of item to choose as the basis for syllabus organisation according to characteristics of our learners has not received much theoretical attention, but Part A of this book contains some interesting practical discussion on the issue.

The second reason why the question of 'unit of organisation' is important is that it opens up the possibility for syllabuses with varying units of organisation. Above it was said that we must select one type of item as our organising principle. This is not of course strictly true, and as long as we do not confuse the student by changing the orientation of the course too often, there is no reason why we should not vary the unit of organisation within the course. In many teaching situations, for example, an attractive possibility is to follow a series of functional units in which a variety of grammatical items is met, with structural units which focus attention on these items and relate them to the grammatical system as a whole. Similarly, there may be good pedagogic reasons for concentrating in some parts of a course on the language appropriate to chosen settings, and on others in language in relation to functions.[5] We might dub this type of syllabus 'multidimensional' to distinguish it from the 'unidimensional syllabus' in which the unit of organisation does not change at all. Indeed, we might see as one of the greatest attractions of *Threshold Level* type inventories, the fact that they can lead to multidimensional syllabuses in which the focus of attention is allowed to change as a course develops.[6]

## 7 The term 'communicative'

In the Introduction to this paper we spoke of the insight which has shaped recent trends in language teaching – that 'being structurally correct' is only a part of what is involved in language ability. It is no acci-

dent that this insight should have occurred when it did, for it reflects a
shift in emphasis which took place within language studies as a whole.
A writer who characterises this shift clearly is the sociolinguist Hymes.
He takes issue with Chomsky and the transformational grammarians
whose view of language competence is very much a grammatical one –
it is knowledge of the language system. To define language competence
in such terms is, Hymes (1970) says, a somewhat 'Garden of Eden'
view for those (like the language teacher) who are concerned with language as a living thing used by individuals and societies. Hymes uses
the term 'communicative competence' to refer to the more general sort
of knowledge and ability native speakers possess. This *includes* knowledge of grammaticality and ability to be grammatical. But it involves
more besides, and Hymes lists several other factors including the factor
of appropriateness mentioned earlier in this paper.

In the most general terms we may say that a 'communicative language teaching' is one which recognises the teaching of 'communicative
competence' as its aim. It is on this level of *aim* that such a language
teaching distinguishes itself from more traditional approaches where the
emphasis is heavily on teaching structural competence. We may thus see
the revision of aims as an *enrichment* – an acceptance that there are
further dimensions of language which need teaching.

We have already seen that one answer to the question of how this
revision and enrichment of aims actually affects the teaching operation
is on the level of syllabus design — the level at which we state our
teaching content. Many, indeed, would use the term 'communicative' as
a synonym for 'notional/functional', to refer to language teaching following a semantic syllabus based on an analysis of students' language
needs. This usage of the term reflects the view discussed earlier in this
paper, that once we are prepared to include items like 'how to ask for a
light' as part of our teaching content, we have half won the battle
against communicative incompetence.

The way we state our teaching content may be half the battle, but the
other half remains to be fought. There is a considerable difference between *stating* that we wish to teach the student 'asking for a light' and
*actually enabling* him to do so in a real communicative situation. We
may begin our teaching operation with a semantic syllabus carefully and
scientifically drawn up to cover the student's communicative needs, yet
utterly fail to teach him how to communicate. If, in other words, we are
to meet our communicative aims, we must give attention to questions of
methodology as well as syllabus design.

The search for a communicative methodology begins with the question 'what does communicative skill involve?'. This issue is given
detailed attention in Part B of this book,[7] but a central point may be
made here. It is that just as at the level of syllabus design the desire to
be communicative has led to an *enrichment* – with more complex syllabus inventories specifying language needs along many dimensions –

there is likely to be a similar effect on the level of methodology. We now see communication as a highly complex skill, involving far more than the sub-skill of 'being grammatical'. Consider for example what is involved in producing a conversational utterance. Apart from being grammatical, the utterance must also be appropriate on very many levels at the same time; it must conform to the speaker's aim, to the role relationships between the interactants, to the setting, topic, linguistic context etc. The speaker must also produce his utterance within severe constraints; he does not know in advance what will be said to him (and hence what his utterance will be a response to) yet, if the conversation is not to flag, he must respond extremely quickly. The rapid formulation of utterances which are simultaneously 'right' on several levels is central to the (spoken) communicative skill. Once we begin to view communication in these terms (rather than simply as the production of structurally correct utterances), then we are posing ourselves exciting methodological problems which it will take new techniques to solve. A communicative methodology will differ significantly from traditional methodology.

## 8 Conclusion

How, then, do the concepts of 'notional', 'functional' on the one hand and 'communicative' on the other relate to each other? It is the relationship of means to end. Our aim is to teach communicative ability, and this may lead us at the syllabus design level to specify and organise our teaching content in a semantic way. Semantic syllabuses are (like all syllabuses) a means to an end – a vehicle for arriving at a destination. But it is also only one means to an end, and we judge a course communicative or otherwise not only (nor even, we might argue, predominantly) in terms of how it is organised, but also in terms of its methodology.

Viewed in this light it is certainly possible to imagine a notional/functional course which, because of its methodology, we would not wish to call communicative. Likewise we may find a structurally-organised course whose methodology practises important aspects of the communicative skill and is thus more worthy of the title 'communicative'. We may certainly argue convincingly that it is easier to reach communicative aims within the framework of a semantic rather than structural syllabus. But the concepts are distinct, and a healthy starting point is to accept that one may 'be notional/functional' without 'being communicative', and even 'be communicative' without 'being notional/functional'.

## Notes

1 Not all contributors to this volume use 'semantic syllabus' as their umbrella term.

Some use the word 'notional', and others speak of 'notional/functional' syllabuses. But despite these differences of terminology it is usually clear what the writers are referring to.

2   This kind of enrichment (for the concept of function) is being given in the field of discourse analysis. See Coulthard (1977) for an introduction to this area of study.

3   *The Concise Oxford Dictionary of Current English*, Ed by Fowler H W and Fowler F G, (O U P)

4   This terminology is not universal. In fact in this volume Alexander uses the word 'proto-syllabus' to describe what is here called a 'syllabus inventory'. Many others use 'syllabus' for 'syllabus inventory' and 'programme' for 'syllabus'! The actual terms used are unimportant, as long as the distinction is somehow made, and it is clear what is being talked about.

5   Johnson and Morrow (1979) and Morrow and Johnson (1979) both use a multi-dimensional syllabus. The latter book provides 'Consolidation Units' at regular intervals, and these contain traditional structural drills.

6   See Michael Swan's paper in this book for a more detailed discussion of the various types of lists possible in a syllabus inventory.

7   See particularly Keith Morrow's paper which considers the processes of conversational interaction in more detail.

# Part A: Applications

# 1 Teaching adult beginners

Though most would agree that a communicative approach has clear application with certain intermediate or advanced students, some would have considerable doubts whether – and if so how – the approach can be used with beginners. The most obvious problem is the fact that beginner students do not yet possess a basic grammatical knowledge. A functionally-organised syllabus seems to imply a lack of grammatical grading, and this, we might feel, will simply confuse the beginner. A second major problem – to some extent present at whatever levels 'general' students are taught, but particularly acute at the beginner level – is how to identify areas of language use which will be of interest to the variety of students within the class.

This section contains three papers written by materials producers all with recent experience in tackling these and other issues associated with the application of a communicative approach at the adult beginner level.

No attempt has been made to persuade or coerce the contributors into putting forward a common view. Rather it was our intention to present a 'forum' where different and sometimes conflicting ideas could be gathered together and compared. The onus is thus very much on the reader to consider critically how the views of the contributors relate to his own situation.

In the first paper, Louis Alexander explicitly mentions the problem of 'marrying' functions and structures, and he describes the various approaches he considered when planning his adult beginner materials. John Milne's paper (written with Tom Jupp) touches on the problem of dealing with the different sorts of learners which any adult beginners' class inevitably contains. In the third paper, Robert O'Neill uses the term 'oblique functionalism' to describe his solution to the problem of being functional at the beginner level. It is a term which captures the spirit of all three papers in this section – the spirit of eclecticism with which the materials producer must approach ideas developed by his more theoretical colleague, the applied linguist.

# LOUIS ALEXANDER[1]

In writing *Mainline Beginners A* and *B* I treated the Council of Europe specifications ( *Waystage* and *The Threshold Level*)[2] as a proto-syllabus for each part of the course. In other words, I attempted to interpret the specifications to evolve the kind of course design which would take into account all the factors implicit in a functional/notional approach. I consciously chose to base my course design on the 'collectively subjective' set of specifications of the Council of Europe than on my own individually subjective intuition, because I believe strongly that a course design should not be merely idiosyncratic. Rather, it should be possible for all and sundry to discern a general principle of organisation. (This certainly used to be the case in a structural approach where many different authors used variations of the same logico-grammatical progression to produce radically different courses.)

The biggest problem by far was to evolve a design at the zero level which would really teach students to do things through language, while at the same time enabling them to master the grammatical structure necessary to achieve this end. One of the silliest misconceptions about a functional/notional approach is that it is supposed to treat grammar in a cavalier fashion. Unless a learner can operate the system he has no chance of achieving the ability to communicate in true social terms and 'operate the system' means controlling the grammar. When a course design is based on one organising principle, all the other elements in it tend to be disorganised. For example, if you organise your course round a structural progression, language functions will tend to be disorganised; if you choose functions as your organising principle, the presentation of grammatical structure is likely to be disorganised. The problem, therefore, was to find a framework which permitted the systematic teaching of communication as well as a coherent and consistent presentation of the necessary structure to go with it. Four models were investigated:

1 *A purely functional model*: i.e. an attempt to teach language functions in some kind of order. It quickly became apparent that this model would rapidly end up as a list, and course designers are not in the business of teaching lists. It also became obvious that there is no one-to-one relationship between function and the way of expressing it. However, valuable insights were gained on the relevance of this model to the organisation of a phrase-book based on slot-and-filler principles. This model can be used at the pre-course level of 'survival' where the concern is simply to provide the student with a repertoire of useful phrases.

2 *A structural/functional model*: i.e. an attempt to interpret the conventional structural progression in functional terms. The first version of *Mainline Beginners* was based on this model but was ultimately rejected when it became clear that functional labels were merely being superimposed on the familiar logico-grammatical progression (e.g. 'Describing

an action that has just occurred' = present perfect.) I have yet to be convinced that this model can truly justify the label 'functional'.

3 *A functional/structural model*: i.e. an attempt to teach a function followed by an investigation of the grammatical content of its exponents. This proved too difficult at the zero level because the grammatical range was too great (e.g. for apologising we immediately arrive at: I'm sorry that + clause; I'm sorry if; I'm sorry for + gerund, etc.). This model was found to be eminently suitable at higher levels and was adopted in Alexander (1973).

4 *'Thematic Areas'*: i.e. topical, functional or notional themes of a very general nature which are basic aspects of everyday life and social communication. (Thematic areas should not be confused with 'centres of interest' such as 'the garage', 'shopping', etc. Such 'themes' would not be general enough to sustain a course design.) After a great deal of trial and error, this was the approach finally adopted and the thematic areas, introduced in *Beginners A* and recycled in *Beginners B*, are as follows:

1 *About you*: the identification of self.
2 *Yourself and others*: the identification of other people.
3 *Please*: requests, offers, suggestions, permission, possibility to do things.
4 *Finding the way*: direction.
5 *Can I?* Possibility, prohibition, necessity, ability, desire to do things.
6 *Where?* Location.
7 *When?* Time.
8 *Describe it!* Information about things, substances and conditions.
9 *I like*: likes, dislikes and preferences.
10 *I want*: wants and needs: people, things and substances.
11 *Doing things*: actions.
12 *Getting things done*: requesting/persuading others to act.

In the course each of these themes is regarded as a major objective within which there are minor objectives, each of which is carefully labelled so that the learner is made aware, at every stage, exactly what he is setting out to achieve. Thus, for Thematic Area 4, we consciously set out to teach the student to find the way in a highly explicit fashion, beginning with the ordinal numbers 'first' to 'fifth', then teaching 'left' and 'right' and then going through each of the following sub-themes:

Direction (location/existence): out of doors, short distances.
Imperatives: out of doors, short distances.
Landmarks.
Location/existence: indoors.
Imperatives and landmarks: indoors.

Out of doors: longer distances.
Mode of transport.
Distance.

Conventional structural grading occurs *within* each thematic area in that 'easy' utterances are taught before 'difficult' ones: e.g.

Where is...? It's... + general and exact directions.
Is there? There's a... + general and exact directions.
Is there? There's one... + general and exact directions.
Where is...? It's... There's a... There's one... + static prepositions.
How can I get to...?/Can you tell me the way to...? + Imperatives, etc.

With discretion, certain utterances (e.g. 'How can I get to...?') are taught 'as formulae' long before they are formally treated. However, there is another kind of 'grading' operating throughout the course: namely, the same situations are periodically re-introduced and become more complex at different levels. An adapted version of this 'thematic area' course design, utilising a six-stage cyclical progression over two years, has been applied in the multi-media course *Follow Me!*[3] so it will be possible to assess its efficacy from different point of view.

Within each thematic area students are made aware of the distinction between receptive and productive language. Many of the activities they are asked to perform involve 'getting the gist' (and therefore coping with authentic or quasi-authentic listening and reading material) as well as 'active production' wholly within their control. The four skills are not rigidly compartmentalised, but students engage in a great variety of language activities: e.g.

Listen and... (respond/assimilate/take notes/report, etc.)
Read and... (take notes, respond, report, etc.)

Settings and social roles are carefully defined. The student is the protagonist throughout and can frequently impose his own choice of language on the teacher. The criterion for choosing likely situations is that they must be relevant in English-as-a-foreign language contexts. (*Not* L1 situations like e.g. 'You are the headmistress of a comprehensive school...') There are frequent opportunities for studying grammatical paradigms as not every part of a paradigm can be adequately practised in a communicative course. Though there is no story-line as such, there is a full-scale accompanying story which is intended to serve as a link-reader between the course and commercially-available controlled reading schemes.

The method can be defined as a three-stage activity from 'grammar-to-communication':

Practice ————⟶ Language in context ————⟶ Improvisation

Under the 'Practice' label the emphasis is on grammatical forms, often out of context, to develop fluency in the learner. ('The rationale of drilling is not that it is a sufficient method for acquiring a language, but that it serves to establish low-level behaviours as habits, thus freeing the conscious mind for higher communicative purposes.'[4]) These forms are then put into a controlled setting (labelled 'Language in context') which provides a rudimentary example of how, when and where, etc., the language which has already been practised is used. This, in turn, prepares the learner for more open-ended communicative activity (labelled 'Improvisation'). Everything the students are learning is constantly brought together in the Improvisation frames, for it is here they are invited to communicate and thus to recall and recombine in entirely new situations, items previously learnt. Improvisation takes two forms: *actual transfer* in which students give true information about themselves and *simulated transfer* in which students are invited to put themselves into straightforward situations, imagining they are using English in likely circumstances within their own countries or abroad.

Improvisation is at the very heart of a methodology based on functional/notional principles: that's what it's all ultimately about. But it poses an acute kind of problem, namely, the need for instructions to set up situations. But this is only critical at the absolute zero level. Soon after, a kind of me-Tarzan-you-Jane way of instructing is possible and English can be used. However, a metalanguage of this kind is also desirable to make students constantly aware of what they are doing and why, so they can actively participate in the learning process.

It is still too early to make value judgements about the functional/notional approach. But one thing is clear: it is here to stay and any course designer writing materials today must be influenced by functional/notional considerations. *Mainline Beginners* is an attempt to apply the principles of this approach at zero level.

## Notes

1 Louis Alexander's adult beginner materials, on which he bases his contribution are *Mainline Beginners*, (Longman, 1978).

2 Van Ek and Alexander (1977), and van Ek (1975).

3 Alexander and Kingsbury (1980).

4 Trim (1977).

# JOHN MILNE[1]

In the winter of 1975/76, we met as a group of authors to write an EFL Course with two broad aims:

(a)  the syllabus of the Course would be arranged on a functional/communicative basis and the students would be encouraged to learn to communicate effectively in English at a simple level from the beginning.

(b)  the students we had in mind would be older teenagers and adults and they would be either complete beginners or beginners in the sense that they had forgotten most of any English which they had ever learned.

To the task of syllabus construction, we brought experience in the design of Spoken English courses for people at work in Britain.[2] For such courses, setting, roles and types of communication can be closely specified. We also used van Ek (1975). We found a serious limitation of this is that it deals only in language exponents at sentence and vocabulary level and avoids two key aspects of real communicative interaction: the extended nature of discourse and speaker intention and hearer interpretation. Furthermore, we soon realised that we could not design a completely functional syllabus for a general group of learners (as defined in (b) above) because a functional approach assumes that the course designer knows what his students want to say, where, and to whom. And this is not possible in a general class where the functional needs of the students vary radically from one person to the next and where many students, especially at beginner level, have no immediate communicative objectives in the outside world at all.

We had, therefore, to make many arbitrary decisions about student objectives, about situations and roles, and about the language used in them. And we experienced a great deal of anxiety and had many doubts about the choices we made. However, we were able to reassure ourselves that the process we were involved in was no more arbitrary than that of the structural syllabus designer when he decides on an order for language structures, and perhaps less so since we were developing much of our material from authentic sources.

Our anxiety and doubts arose not only because there was no received wisdom on the designing of functional/communicative courses, but also because there are many more variables to take account of than in a structural approach, which is essentially one dimensional. Any language course syllabus must specify the linguistic forms of the language to be mastered, but in a functional/communicative approach these linguistic items are only one strand in a multi-dimensional syllabus and they are specified last in the process of material writing rather than first.

Also, we realised that a functional/communicative approach to language learning requires a rejection of a simplistic behaviourist view of language acquisition as primarily a process of repetition and habit formation. In pursuing a functional/communicative approach, we found ourselves taken back to first principles and forced to challenge many assumptions about textbook writing and about language learning.

I outline below some of the problems we faced and I indicate briefly how we went about trying to provide solutions to these problems.

## 1 The textbook and the language learning process

There are a number of contradictions between what a textbook can offer a student and what the student needs in order to learn to communicate effectively in English. The textbook tends to equate learning with teaching. Obviously there is a correlation between the two, but the strength of the correlation depends upon the individual learner. Most textbooks seem to suggest that learners can all learn the same things in the same way and at the same pace. To avoid this we tried to include as much variety and choice as possible in the presentation and analysis of language and in the methods and techniques of language practice.

What each learner wants and chooses to learn – especially as far as items of vocabulary are concerned at beginner level – is individual to that learner. But the textbook imposes a standard, unified stock of language on all the students who use it. This is especially demotivating for adult students who may want to know particular items of language; for example, vocabulary items connected with their work or with their leisure activities. We therefore encourage students from the beginning to learn additional material by featuring a Do-It-Yourself-Section – D I Y. These sections provide students with varied strategies for asking for those words and expressions which they themselves want to learn. Also, in these sections we try to latch on to the use of English in the learner's environment. In most countries of the world, examples of English can be found in hotels, in restaurants, in airport lounges, on electrical goods, on packaged food and drink of all sorts, on radio and TV, and on magazine stalls. In the D I Y sections, we make the learners aware that there are many English words around them, we suggest places where such words may be found, and we ask the learners to go and look for them.

A textbook is a printed document and this blurs the distinction between the material in the book which is meant to be read and the material which is meant to be listened to. Even worse, it may suggest to teachers and to students that there are no differences between spoken and written English. We try to avoid this blurring of the distinctions between written and spoken language by offering some independent development of the skills. Students soon learn that they are expected to be able to listen to more than they themselves can produce in speech and to read more than they can write. Also many of the reading passages are based on authentic material and the language in them can be seen to be different from the language used in the dialogue.

## 2  Varieties of English

We tend to forget that when we speak of 'the English language' we are speaking of an abstraction – an idealised synthesis of numberless ideolects. But the textbook tends to impose on those who use it a standardised, unified model of English. This contradiction raises a number of problems.

The language used varies according to the situation the speakers are in, and according to their roles and relationships. But it would be totally confusing at the beginner stage to present in a textbook the host of phonological, lexical, grammatical and stylistic variations which may be significant in different settings and which may occur as roles and relationships are changed. Many would argue that this cannot be done at all – students must learn the significance of these variations when they meet them in real life. But this leads back to the theory of adaptation – teach the students the linguistic system and they will learn to adapt it as and when such adaptation is required. By undertaking to write a course whose main aim is to enable the students to communicate effectively, we have explicitly rejected this theory of adaptation.

The compromise solution we present is to emphasise the difference between the *productive* and *receptive* abilities. We give the students a standard model for production, but students are expected to be able to understand much more than they can produce and the material for receptive understanding shows the possibility of variety in language use. Beyond this, we introduce the idea of variation only at a very broad level of analysis – for example, contrasts between written and spoken English, and some differences between the language we use in formal and in informal situations.

The language we use also varies according to age, occupation and interests. We assume that the students will be in their late teens or early twenties. They will live in a European tradition and will be reasonably aware of the world around them. These assumptions affected the choice of language we present as a model for production, the choice of the different characters in the Course who use that language, the choice of the situations these characters find themselves in, and the selection of games, songs and other classroom activities.

But while making these generalised assumptions, we still kept in mind the fact that each learner is an individual with his own needs and his own interests. To encourage this individuality, we have made the language practice activities open-ended wherever possible. We give examples of how to talk about certain subjects, but we encourage the students to turn the subject of conversation to what interests them.

## 3 Content

Because in many traditional courses the learning task has been seen in mechanistic terms, EFL course books have tended to stress the trivial and the entertaining in their content. New EFL courses are supposedly made original and exciting by designers and artists and so they have become another consumer item which is principally distinguished by its packaging. We wanted very much to include some genuine content which would be informative, educational and stimulating. But once again the fact that we were writing a *general* course meant that we were faced with a host of problems in connection with content, and these problems, together with commercial pressures, push the writer towards the 'international culture' of English. While this is logical, it has to be remembered that, for most learners, situations arising out of this 'international culture' have very little cultural or social reality. They are largely a 'cellophane secondary reality' created by magazines, records and film and TV.

We accept that an EFL course should reflect English as the language of international culture, but, at the same time, the learner should be equipped from an early stage with the language needed to examine and criticise this culture. Moreover, learning a language should be a personal experience which opens up a world of ideas, which extends the understanding of language as such, and which creates an opportunity for personal travel, for reading, for study and for relationships in English-speaking countries or with English-speaking visitors.

## 4 Syllabus design

We took as our starting point three very broad themes reflecting different aspects of communication:

talking about yourself as an individual
talking about physical surroundings and things
interaction by language between the individual and his environment

We assumed that these themes could be tackled at a fairly superficial level in a beginner course – hence the title: *Encounters*.

The contexts and situations were chosen to reflect the three themes and are arranged to provide a progression from the simple to the more complex. The contexts were based either on fictional situations and characters, or on real examples of written language use, modified as necessary.

The language functions were chosen because they are needed in the situations we had selected, and further functions were included for immediate use in the classroom itself. The particular examples of the functions were selected on the basis of their range of use and of linguistic simplicity and structural grading. The emphasis upon language function means that a learner can communicate in English and understand the usefulness of what he is learning from the very beginning of the course.

The structural syllabus of the course developed out of the examples of the language functions. But, since we often chose the particular examples on the basis of linguistic simplicity, we did, to this extent, impose a structural syllabus on them. However, we also permitted particular examples of a language structure to occur before they were dealt with systematically and in some cases there are examples of productive language which are never dealt with structurally, but are treated throughout as fixed phrases.

The process of syllabus design was, therefore, one of continually choosing and modifying both forms and functions so that they fit together and represent as useful and as simple a progression for the learner as possible. The final language syllabus consists of one syllabus of transactions and functions and one syllabus of structures and the structural syllabus is generally subservient to the purposes of the functional one.

## Notes

1   T C Jupp collaborated on the writing of this paper. The materials described in it are Garton-Sprenger, J, Jupp, T C, Milne J, Prowse, P, *Encounters*, (Heinemann Educational Books, 1979).

2   Some of this experience will be found in Jupp and Hodlin (1975).

# ROBERT O'NEILL[1]

I am going to argue here for what I shall call 'oblique functionalism'. I shall explain what I mean. And I shall argue that it is oblique functionalism rather than the more explicit variety that often – not always – best serves the needs of many adult learners in the elementary and intermediate stages.

Oblique functionalism, as I shall show, has the same final, ultimate aims as the more explicit variety. That is, it can be justified only in terms of what it ultimately helps the learner *to do with the language*. Can he state something and make it clear that it is only an opinion, open to argument? Can she use the language to make him expand upon the argument and give reasons? Can they both use the language effectively to disagree, and to suggest a meal or a drink afterwards? Can they, after deciding where to go, stop a passer-by, ask for instructions about how to get there, and understand the reply? Can they understand the menu when they get there or ask the waiter to explain what they do not understand? And can they after being overcharged write an appropriate letter of complaint to the head office of the organisation of which the restaurant is a part?

But these are terminal objectives. And terminal objectives are not the same thing as the strategies for attaining them, the steps along the way. Oblique functionalism does not insist, as does the more aggressive variety of explicit functionalism, that each of these steps should be clearly labelled in functional terms. It recognises that a great deal of a course with explicit functional aims cannot always be made explicit at the time it is first presented. Obliquely functional materials may take what at times appear to be detours into areas of the language that have no explicit functional description. However, at the end of the course, these areas must be shown to be central to the learner's communicative competence, essential for a whole variety of communicative operations relevant to the learner's needs.

Let me describe some of the audiences or groups of learners for whom obliquely functional approaches are in my opinion more useful. Then I shall describe some of the strategies involved.

1 There are some groups of adult beginners who seem to have mainly social rather than linguistic motivation. They are in the group at least as much for each other's company as they are for the language. This is particularly true of some evening classes abroad.

The strategies and materials for such courses must reflect the group's social motivation and enhance it. This is not always in conflict with the functional aims of the course, but neither is it always directly compatible. Many of the things done in the class cannot and need not be shown to be essential for the functional aims of the course. Some of these things may only promote simple interaction between members of the group.

Such groups are sometimes dismissed as not being 'serious'. I profoundly disagree. Such an attitude overlooks one of the most basic reasons for learning a language or making use of it afterwards.

2   Some groups are composed of adults with rather vague notions that English may be useful to them in their jobs or the next time they go to the London sales. These may again be evening classes abroad. It is possible to identify a number of potentially relevant functional goals for them. But time constraints – the group may meet only 30 times a year for one-and-a-half-hour sessions – make it extremely difficult to realise these goals except at a very superficial and trivial level. For such groups it is often better to select a few basic structures with wide functional cover or relevance and concentrate upon them. I shall come back to this point later.

3   All over the world there are groups of adult beginners whose psychological barriers you must first penetrate before you can teach effectively or create good learning conditions. The group may have many individuals in it who have tried to learn the language before without much success. Their sensitivity and receptivity to language has to be reawakened. Or the group may have extremely traditional expectations of what learning a language involves. They may be reluctant even to look at or interact with each other. Unless the teacher spends as much time coping with these barriers at first and breaking them down as he or she does on direct functional teaching, resistance continues to build up. Eventually an impasse is reached. The strategies for overcoming them often have no explicit functional justification and need none. But teachers may be reluctant to undertake them because it may not seem to them or their colleagues like 'real language teaching'.

4   There are many other groups – perhaps these are most common of all – made up of individuals whose functional needs and interests conflict either in priority or nature. In one small group of adult beginners there may be a young man interested primarily in chatting up women, a very intellectual girl who wants to discuss politics all the time and is impatient of more mundane things, an immigrant entrepreneur who wants the language of negotiation, haggling and quoting prices, a presessional student who has to learn how to follow lectures in a particular discipline and someone employed in a tourist-agency in Paris or Dusseldorf whose most pressing needs are to understand telex messages in English and deal with the limited number of questions English-speaking tourists ask most frequently.

With luck you may be able to identify a core of functional items essential for all. But each has needs that will be perceived by the others as either irrelevant or far-from-urgent. If you are too explicit about the specific application of any one functional item, everyone turns off except the one individual who sees the item as directly related to her or his needs.

What are the solutions which both satisfy the disparate and sometimes competing needs of the various groups I have described and at the same time lead finally to clearly-defined functional objectives?

First, I think it essential for adult beginners of the types I have described to identify not only a core syllabus of functions but also a core syllabus of language structures which can be used to realise them. Just as you must limit the first, so you can and must limit the second. There is sometimes a bit of difficult horse-trading involved, but it is an inescapable and necessary process. What if an essential function is identified that requires language outside the core structural syllabus? There are several answers. One is to see if there is some way of realising it below the generative-structure level; it may only be a phrase or an accepted language formulae like 'Please' or 'If you don't mind', which can be learned globally. The other answer is to decide which members of the group most need this function, and to provide the language necessary in self-study or tutoring sessions with them. Such a strategy allows you to go well beyond the core for various individuals yet not to burden the receptive and assimilative faculties of the others who need the language less urgently or not at all.

This last strategy implies a certain reorganisation of our traditional concept of the language lesson or chunk of time alloted to a class in an intensive language course. It means that a certain proportion of time – at least 15 minutes out of an individual lesson or a whole hour out of a six-hour day is given up to these self-study or individual tutoring activities. And it also implies the necessary resources for each group; short readers, individual practice materials, visual materials laid aside for this kind of use. In fact, of course, it is not a radical departure at all. It is what village schoolmistresses frequently did a century ago!

The second solution is, again, not a radical departure from what many teachers and course-designers already do. It involves the concept of the spiral, or concentricity. But it involves it in a slightly new way. The core structures are rotated at intervals with the core functions. 'Can', for example, may first be introduced to express ability or possibility ('I can swim but I can't ski.'). Later it is practised as a request form ('Can you type this letter for me, please?'). After yet another interval it can be used as a means of asking permission ('Can I leave now?'). Each time the structure is linked to a core function. Each rotation allows the learner another chance to master the basic structure and to apply it in a particular communicative setting. At various times throughout the course, the structure is revised within all the functions it has been used. This allows revision not just of the structure but, more importantly, a review of the functional repertoire acquired by the learner. At this point, alternative ways of realising some of the functions can be introduced. And these may go beyond the core structural syllabus itself.

The third solution is the concept of what I can call only 'peripheral focus'. Suppose you are teaching a group of foreign technicians how to give operating instructions for the procedures and tools they use in their work. But they all use different tools in different procedures. One is a welder. The other a bench-lathe operator. The third is a pipe-fitter. Instead of choosing one central tool or procedure from the work of any one of the three, you deliberately take something on the periphery of all their work, or perhaps quite outside it. For example, you may teach them sequencing markers ('First ... Then ... After that ... Finally ...') by illustrating and getting them to illustrate a common gadget like a cassette recorder, or even the telephone. You do this not because you suppose anyone will want to explain to someone else how to use a recorder or a phone, but because the language involved is common to all sequencing operations but not particular to any of your three technicians. And you do it because *this forces the technicians to transfer the language to their own particular operations*! Getting them to make the transfer themselves rather than presenting the language to them in a form they can immediately use is often a far more effective channel into their long-term memories and generative repertoires.

The fourth solution is already common practice amongst those involved in functional teaching. Information-gap, 'ask each other' and various forms of role-taking exercise are used not only in order to practise specific language points but also to promote maximum interaction among the group. The group must generate its own impetus, cohere together, help each other, and become interested in each other's individual backgrounds, goals and personalities. This is essential for almost all language-learning groups, and not just those with primarily social motivations.

The fifth solution is in some ways part of the first. It goes under the name of 'internal differentiation'. Almost from the beginning, individuals within each group will progress at different rates. And so there must be an outer and an inner ring in the core syllabus. The inner ring is, if you like, the core of the core. It represents the minimal functional and structural competence the different members of the group need to communicate with each other. One student may have only one request form. Another may acquire several, appropriate for different tenors or registers. Both must have at least one basic request form and means of responding to it for ordinary classroom interaction.

The sixth solution is the most neglected, I think, in mainstream functional and structural teaching. It seems the least clearly relevant to explicit functional goals. And yet it is probably the most essential of all the solutions. And it is the one about which I must, because of lack of space and my own ignorance, speak the most superficially. How do we awaken and increase receptivity to language? Two rich arsenals of strategies and techniques for doing this are the two methods called 'The Silent Way' and 'Suggestopedia'. The works of Gattegno and Lozanov must be referred to in depth for this. I know of no better, brief introduction to the ideas than the section devoted to both in Stevick (1976).

The techniques from both can be combined with functional teaching, as long as we do not insist that each step is clearly identified in functional terms. Under what functional heading does 'increasing receptivity' come?

Oblique functionalism does not select structural items because they are part of the whole grammatical system but because they are essential if the learner is to attain specific functional goals. Oblique functionalism recognises that there are limits to what a particular individual can learn in a certain time. It deliberately uses the structural techniques of selection, progression and concentricity in order to develop the learner's generative repertoire with the language. But many of the items that traditionally occur in a structural syllabus will never occur in an obliquely functional one. Such a syllabus uses selection and progression but subordinates them to clearly-defined functional objectives. However, in order to attain those terminal objectives, an obliquely functional approach will use many strategies and techniques with no immediate short-term but with very real long-term functional relevance.

## Note

1   R O' Neill's adult beginners materials are *Kernel One*, (Longman, 1979).

# 2 Teaching other types of beginner

This section contains two papers. In the first, Nicolas Hawkes considers some of the problems involved in using a communicative approach for the teaching of primary school pupils, and in the course of his discussion he looks at possible solutions for the teaching of pupils in a variety of educational settings. The second paper, by Michael Swan, is concerned with an increasingly common and particularly problematic type of student – the 'faux débutant' or false beginner.

At the beginning of his paper Hawkes asks three questions. The first of these indicates a similarity in the problems faced by primary and adult beginner materials producers. 'Is,' Hawkes asks, 'a communicative approach to L2 learning likely to be *intrinsically* unsuitable to Primary pupils, if they are beginners and if their exact needs for it are not foreseeable?' Similar issues were faced by the writers in Section 1.

Hawkes's answer to his question is no and in this respect the tone of his article is more positive towards a communicative approach than Swan's. But despite this difference of emphasis, both writers share with each other (and with the writers in Section 1) the same spirit of eclecticism. This is clearly revealed in the final paragraphs of both articles, which warn against the dangers of dogma. There should, Hawkes says, 'be no cry that "structural patterns are now out".' The sentiment is echoed by Swan who, while conceding advantages to a communicative approach, warns that 'it would be a pity if . . . . . the new approach became a strait jacket'.

# NICOLAS HAWKES[1]  Primary children

Proposals for placing second-language teaching on a communicative basis have been put forward[2] on general theoretical grounds concerning language and learning. Most illustrations of this approach have taken the learners' *foreseeable communicative needs* in the second language (L2) as the foundation of syllabus and teaching materials.[3] Attention has therefore been focussed on those older learners whose position in education or employment allows their L2 needs to be foreseen. It may naturally be wondered whether a communicative approach has anything to offer to second-language teaching to Primary School children who are too young to know what languages, for what purposes, they will require in future.

In recent years, and independently of developments in Applied Linguistics, there has been much re-thinking of assumptions about language-teaching for young children. In the U.S.A. there has been a spate of Bilingual Education programmes, mainly for children of minority language groups.[4] Foreign-language teaching in Primary schools is expanding in Europe, although in Britain there is less enthusiasm than there was.[5] In many African countries, language policy and practice in Primary education is in constant flux.[6] Everywhere policy is usually debated in terms of learners' age *per se*, but one may rather approach the matter in the other direction, and ask: how can the learning of an L2 be made most attractive and relevant to young children, granted their age and cultural setting?[7] The well-established notion that it is an advantage to start young may perhaps be converted into social reality only if syllabuses, materials and methods for the age-group are re-examined. It is to this point that ideas from linguistics can most usefully be applied, especially if they are in harmony with general educational principles which have already, in some cases, been successfully adapted to an L2 situation.

In particular, one may ask 3 questions:

1 Is a communicative approach to L2 learning likely to be *intrinsically* unsuitable to Primary pupils, if they are beginners and if their exact needs for it are not foreseeable?

2 Indeed, is it always essential that a communicative approach should rest on assumptions about learners' *future needs* in L2?

3 Is one bound to the belief that a closely-specified communicative *syllabus* must precede materials development and new methods?

It is argued here that all 3 answers should be No, and evidence will be adduced from experience of 2 materials development projects, one for European children of 9–11, the other in Anglophone Africa, for 6–12 year olds.

So far from being intrinsically unsuitable to young pupils, an approach which does not separate the teaching of a language from communicative contexts can only be right for them. Infants communicate before they speak, and to the young child it is unnatural, and cognitively difficult, to abstract 'language' from the purposes for which it is used. This principle applies as much to L2 as to L1. It is particularly unsound to teach Primary children in ways superficially adapted from Secondary school, for this is likely to be unsuccessful in itself, and to lead to the crushing of interest when the Secondary course proves to be a remedial re-run of the Primary one.

If, in relation to question 2, it has been decided on principle to teach an L2 in certain Primary schools, then a selective basis for communicative syllabus[8] or materials can be sought in *the children's experience of communicating in L1*, adapted to the rest of the curriculum in character and content. Language-teaching to young children cannot simply be a reflex of the socio-linguistic profile of the wider community, or of adult estimates of their future needs.

Lastly, at these ages, it is the concrete activities and situations in which L2 is presented which are all-important. It is therefore artificial to separate syllabus from materials, and materials development from classroom use. Though the bias of this paper is that of a materials writer, we take it as ideal that there should be close coordination among syllabus planners, materials writers, artists, designers and teachers, no rigid precedence being granted to the former. The guiding principle assumed here for a communicative approach to syllabuses or teaching materials is that one moves from aims and ideas about content to the selection of language needed to express the content, and not (as in a structural course) from a language syllabus to the selection of examples and of contexts in which to present them. In our first case, of European 9–11 year-olds learning English, a major aim was to develop closer links between foreign language-teaching and the curriculum generally,[9] which itself was seen as being integrated and environmental in character. The choice of curriculum content to be the basis for language learning will tend to vary with local circumstances, and be more difficult to make if Primary education retains its traditional subject-barriers and authoritarian teaching style. *Kaleidoscope* is an international course, trialled in several countries. Hence the writers were not bound to any one syllabus, but had to be flexible enough for the material to be viable in, for example, both Sweden and Italy. An account of its writing has already been published[10] so we will only refer here to 3 types of unit in the course: a) units in which approximate equivalence was assumed between the learners' language experience and that of British or American children of the same age e.g. arguing about possessions, playground activities, giving directions, talking about hobbies and sports. Clearly this principle could only operate because applied within one broadly defined cultural area; b) units in which the L2 is linked to other-subject learning;

c) units in which the L2 is taught to function as a medium of teacher control and of general classroom activities (borrowing, drawing, team games, etc.). Examples may briefly be set out thus:

| | TOPIC | ACTIVITY | TEXT |
|---|---|---|---|
| 1 | Hobbies | Autograph collecting | Can I have your autograph please? Yes, here you are./Sorry I haven't got time. |
| 2 | Time | Talking about time-zones with a globe. | What time is it here/in (Washington)? It's (2) o'clock in the (morning). |
| 3 | Where? | Claiming possession. | That's my (book). No, it isn't. It's mine. |

Planning and writing was done as from left to right in the table.[11] The results of the creative process must constantly be modified, re-ordered or rejected in the light of language factors such as total load, number of new items occurring, and relation to previous items. Linguistic planning and control in a communicative course, so far from being neglected, requires all the more care and labour just because it is not derived from a neat structural syllabus. The overall outcome in this case fell mainly within the linguistic range covered by current structure-based courses[12] but differing in: certain lexical peculiarities; greater variety of items per unit; less predictable language sequence; omission of such structural niceties as question-tags; a smaller total of items in relation to teaching time. Age, cultural context and general educational priorities influence content more than purely linguistic considerations. In van Ek's terms[13] topics and specific notions play a larger part than language function as such.

Indeed, the role of communicative functions, such as 'denial' or 'expression of tolerance' is not as fundamental as might be expected. To label and select utterances in these terms, and present them in a functional syllabus to which writers and teachers are then bound[14] may be as much a process of abstraction and interference with natural use of language as is found in a structural syllabus.[15] A series of lexically different exchanges in which 'denials' are made may seem quite arbitrary, compared with the real unity of subject-matter or situation. Primary-level teaching materials of this kind are therefore likely to be communicative in general character rather than building up a communicative competence by systematic steps. Except for certain social formulae, short-term mastery is not sought; the approach is gradual, cyclic and non-intensive.

Some comment should be made here on the question of authenticity of the teaching text.[16] It might be thought that the language of arguing about possessions, or autograph collecting, for example, should be taught as derived directly from recordings of native-speakers of the same age. Indeed, the writers of *Kaleidoscope* had available to them quantities of verbatim recordings of British children's topical discussions, in the materials of the York Child Language Survey.[17] But it was very difficult to use because of the sheer quantity of the native utterance in relation to each communicative event, and of disconnectedness and frequent inconsequence. They at least required extensive editing[18] into something still authentic-sounding, but briefer, more explicit and more introductory in character, free from the pre-suppositions natural to the speech of native-speakers who know each other. There is another and more fundamental difficulty too, concerning the underlying aims of a Primary language course. To invoke the criterion of pure authenticity is surely to imply a desire for native-like competence within the scope of the course, or at least an ability to comprehend native speech *in situ*. This may sometimes be the case, but often it is not. Normally, the Primary level is *preparatory* to later levels of teaching, which may then perhaps aim at native-like command. Target utterances in a Primary course must sound natural to the native ear, but must also be understandable in the learning situation, at the expense (if necessary) of being replicas of native utterances. The learners' quantitative limits are a constant factor in L2 learning, independent of whether syllabus and materials are structural or communicative.

A quite distinct approach to the selection of communicative contexts is required if the L2 functions as an educational medium and national language, though not itself indigenous, as in the case of English in African countries where it is taught from the beginning of Primary schooling for some years before it becomes the medium of instruction. Whether it is a subject only, or the medium[19] there is often a need to make the teaching of English more active and more real to children, many of whom have failed to acquire a functional command of it from the mechanical drills and steeply-graded, artificial 'passages' through which the language is frequently taught. The challenge to syllabus design and methodology is important and difficult, for English there has a central educational role, far from the native setting in which its communicative patterns have been shaped. The linguistic forms themselves are not in question; there is as yet no authoritative demand for the explicit teaching of regional variants. But insofar as the 'rules of speaking' for children are conceived differently in, for example, Nigeria or Kenya from the conceptions that apply in the average British or Dutch classroom, there are bound to be cultural implications in the teaching of English on a communicative basis which do not appear in most structural courses. Thus a dilemma faces the Primary course-writer in seeking to impart 'communicative English'; is he to base the oral language on native-English conventions, and risk being culturally alien, or on indigenous L1 conventions, and risk patterns of usage which are alien to English? Either might be better than so neutralising the language that it lacks any functional force at all.

In the present writer's experience of a West African project,[20] only a series of *ad hoc* decisions and compromises will produce an acceptable overall course, but the resolving of the dilemma should favour the L1 conventions, of home, school and children's play. Policy on the use of indigenous languages for education is rightly opposed to English being taught with other-subject content, and this reduces the possibilities for integration of that kind.

Some examples are now briefly listed to show how speech may need adjustment to cultural norms, especially in dialogue and question-and-answer activities:

a)  Who speaks first? e.g. Would a child greet his senior or wait to be addressed?

b)  Does one speak at all? e.g. Would a farmer explain a hoeing technique to his son, or expect him to learn by watching?

c)  What questions are disrespectful? e.g. Would a child ask his teacher 'Are you a teacher?' (as in another published course)

d)  Superficial politeness of English *wording*: e.g. Would a driver call out 'Excuse me *please*' to a young girl?

e)  Assumptions about maturity: e.g. Would a 9-year-old engage in 'market dialogue' with a trader?

f)  Assumptions about independence of mind; e.g. where relevant to problem-solving as a language activity.

It may be objected that presenting English as if it were normally used in a West African market, farm or family home is wholly artificial. But this is to miss the psychological point for the child starting English at 6 or 7. There is no functionally valid alternative to building L2 learning on his L1 experience. Rather than asking if every classroom activity is a rehearsal for the children's lives, the overriding aim should be motivation and maximum clarity in relation to what they already know. The set 'passage' communicates nothing, and is most of all divorced from any reality. This has allowed course-writers to pile on new words and structures, thus enlarging the task while removing the motive. Both faults are avoided by the use of communicative texts, drawing upon everyday life, with a reduced language load and more active methods.

In a similar project in the Gulf,[21] a writing and publishing team have developed richly varied communicative materials within the rather different cultural policy laid down, by which English is seen from the beginning as a potential link with the non-Arab world. This is directly reflected in the texts and characters of the course which is provided with a substantial pack of aids in support of the communicative activities.

The case of minority group children in Britain provides a counter-example to the West African one. For them, English is the language of the wider community, the 'second language', and L2 teaching should surely be based on natural points of contact with it. Even where the minority tends to be socially separate, it is relatively easy to estimate the English communicative needs of even the youngest children. Indeed, the SCOPE materials are a blend of this approach with structural teaching.[22] More recently, teachers trained and experienced in the best practices of progressive mother-tongue education in Britain have reported successful adaptations of them to L2 teaching,[23] similar to what is being proposed here. A major element in this minority-group context is the initial teaching of reading in English. This is also important for African children whose own languages are as yet undeveloped in reading and reading-teaching materials.[24] But for the older *Kaleidoscope* pupils, English reading and writing is taught in incidental ways reflecting children's own reading and writing (such as instructions in kits, magazine literature, postcards, and short letters to relatives) rather than being a formal exercise in which the same non-communicative sentences are cycled through the 4 skills of listening, speaking, reading and writing.

The implications of a communicative approach for methodology have been implicit in this discussion of syllabus and course construction. The emphasis is on activities, dialogues, true-for-me statements, genuine questions and genuine answers, games with a point, and songs that you can enjoy. It is vitally important that method should be taken into account in the planning of syllabus and materials. If it is not, the teacher may be left with no time to do more than teach fixed dialogues for memorisation. However communicative the target texts may be, they will lose their point unless the teaching method allows the learner himself to sense their functional value.

Though we have simplistically contrasted 'communicative' with 'structural' teaching, it would be wrong and unnecessary to assume that there must be a stark antithesis between language-controlled 'structural' courses and linguistically haphazard 'communicative' ones. A communicative course may provide for formal presentation and practice of structural and lexical items before they are incorporated into the dialogue (or other context) which required their inclusion in the first place. It may also provide for formal revision of such items after they have occurred in several separate contexts. There should be no dogma about this, and no cry that 'structural patterns are now "out"'. Learning a language is not only a matter of learning to communicate in that language. If current interest in a communicative approach can avoid a 'bandwagon effect', then its influence is more likely to be long-lasting, and to make the teaching of second-languages to young children more successful and more enjoyable, in many different educational settings.

## Notes

1   This paper is based mainly on the writer's experience in co-authoring *Kaleidoscope* 1–3 (Macmillan Education 1976–7), and editing and co-authoring *Nigeria Primary English* (Longman Nigeria, 1979 onwards).

2   E.g. Wilkins (1973).

3   Materials as for example described in Allen and Widdowson (1974).

4   See Alatis and Twaddell (1976).

5   cf. Burstall et al (1974).

6   Hawes (1979), pp. 76–81, 111.

7   See Stern (1976).

8   The use of the word 'communicative' for 'semantic' or 'notional/functional' is quite common (eds.).

9   cf. Stern (1972).

10   Wright and Betteridge (1976); Hawkes (1974).

11   See Levine (1973).

12   See the analysis carried out in Broughton (1972).

13   van Ek (1978), p. 23.

14   cf. Munby (1978), p. 218.

15   As Brumfit (1978) has pointed out.

16   See Widdowson (1976).

17   Transcripts of recordings by R Hasan and R J Handscombe, with associated occasional papers by Handscombe and Rutherford, Nuffield Foundation/University of York 1965 onwards.

18   cf. Davies (1973).

19   See Hawkes (1976).

20   Hawkes et al (1979).

21   O'Neill and Snow (1977).

22   Derrick et al (1969).

23   E.g. Gutale (1975); Garvie (1976).

24   cf. Hawkes and Bezanson (1976).

# MICHAEL SWAN   False beginners

Attitudes to language syllabus design have changed a good deal over the
last ten years or so. Linguists have become increasingly interested in
'language in use', rather than in language as a formal system. At the
same time, the aims of language teaching have become more practical:
the older concern with an all-purpose mastery of a foreign language is
giving way to a desire to teach a working knowledge of a language for
clearly definable purposes. The linguist's analyses of language in communicative terms, and the educationalist's interest in communicative
competence, have coincided to favour the production of new kinds of
language syllabuses and language-teaching materials. The results have
often been lively and exciting, and there is no doubt that considerable
progress has been made in teaching methodology. Inevitably, perhaps,
this progress has been accompanied by a rejection of previous
approaches to language teaching, and of the (often unsatisfactory) materials and attitudes associated with them. In this paper, I wish to suggest
that the current rejection of the 'conventional wisdom' is largely mis-
taken, that it involves a serious misunderstanding of the principles of
language syllabus design, and that narrowly 'communicative' syllabuses
are unlikely to be any more effective than earlier types of syllabus. At
lower levels, indeed, they may be a good deal less effective, and later
in the paper I shall consider the special case of 'faux débutants'. First of
all, however, I should like to discuss the question of language syllabus
design in more general terms.

Criticism of earlier language-teaching approaches often focuses on the
structural framework of the courses. The argument tends to go as follows: 'In the bad old days, language courses were organised around a
structural syllabus. In such courses, students were taught the forms of
the language, but they did not learn the meanings or communicative use
of these forms'. Nowadays, things are different. We start from a semantic syllabus,[1] which categorises the language in terms of meanings and
communicative functions, and we relate the forms to these meanings.
According to this view, 'structural' syllabuses and 'communicative' or
'semantic' syllabuses are incompatible alternatives; of the two, semantic
syllabuses are preferable.

If it is true (and this is debatable) that most older approaches tended
to emphasise form at the expense of meaning, there is some evidence
that the opposite is now happening. (It is interesting that, in the index to
Munby (1978), there are no entries for *grammar* or *structure*.) We are
certainly getting a good deal better at teaching students to use language
forms in ways appropriate to their purposes; it is not clear that we are
making a very good job of helping them to learn the forms themselves.
Part of the trouble arises from the belief that there is such a thing as a
single syllabus (structural, or communicative, or other) which can be
used as the basis of a language teaching programme. This is not the

case. There are various syllabuses, corresponding to the various points of view from which language can be described, and a language programme will contain elements drawn from some or all of them. These syllabuses include the following:

1  *A phonological syllabus.* Examples of items that might be included: how to pronounce [θ]; how to distinguish /s/ and /z/; weak forms; contrastive high pitch.
2  *A lexical syllabus.* Examples of possible items: *tall*, *guitar*, *relax*, *dashboard*.
3  *A structural syllabus.* Possible items: prepositions with points of time; the 'present progressive' with future reference; *some* and *any*.
4  *A notional syllabus.* Possible items: how to refer to points of time; how to talk about the future; how to refer to the instrument with which an action is performed.
5  *A functional syllabus.* Possible items: how to warn; how to express enthusiastic appreciation; how to borrow things.
6  *A topic syllabus.* Possible items: the language used to talk about marriage and divorce; the parts of a car.
7  *A situational syllabus.* Possible items: what to say when shopping; how to answer the phone.
8  *A discourse syllabus.* Possible items: the use of intonation as a floor-holding device; how to break into a conversation; boundary-markers in speech and writing.
9  *A rhetorical syllabus.* Possible items: summarising; writing business letters; organising an essay.
10  *A stylistic syllabus.* Possible items: levels of politeness; degrees of formality; poetic word-order.
11  *A 'cultural background' syllabus.* Possible items: British humour; the American electoral system; nursery rhymes.

Obviously, we shall not give equal importance to each of these syllabuses in all kinds of course, but the first seven, at least, will be essential components of most language teaching programmes. The syllabuses clearly overlap, but no one of them can completely include or replace any of the others. At first sight, we might feel that syllabuses 4–7 on the list, taken together, will predict all the words that students will need, so that a separate lexical syllabus will become redundant. This appears plausible, but it is not in fact so. The reason is that syllabuses like 4–7 can only be relied on to throw up words that are closely tied to the topics, notion/functions or situations that appear in the syllabus. Other, more 'general-purpose' words are likely to be overlooked. Thus, we can expect syllabuses of this kind to list words and expressions like *o'clock* (semantico-grammatical category of 'point of time'), *look out*! (functional category of 'warning'), *speaking* (situational category of 'telephoning') or *dashboard* (topic category of 'parts of a car'). But none of these syllabuses is certain to tell us that a particular group of students may need to learn the words *relax*, *easy*, *yellowish*, *remote* or *importance*. General-purpose vocabulary of this kind tends to fall through the notional/functional/topic/situational net, and is more reliably handled by traditional methods such as the use of word-frequency counts.

The same argument holds good for structures. In practice, semantic syllabuses include much the same structures as traditional grammatical syllabuses (so that a semantic syllabus and a structural syllabus may both relate *at* to points of time, or *going to* to the future – but in opposite directions, so to speak). However, the two lists are not identical. There are structural features of English which foreigners need to learn, but which do not carry much 'notional/functional' meaning — for instance, some features of word-order, or the sentence-patterns used with particular verbs. These points tend to be left out of semantic syllabuses (but are no easier to learn than other structural points), and one needs to consult an old-style structure list to be sure that one's grammar programme is complete.

To ask whether a structural or semantic syllabus is 'better' is like asking 'Shall I practise scales or play the Mendelssohn concerto?' The two things are simply not in competition. A semantic syllabus describes the language at a higher level of organisation than a structural syllabus – a level where words and structures are already combined into communicative acts. A coherent syllabus at this level is a very valuable thing to have, and semantic descriptions make it possible to approach the teaching of language use in a more systematic way than before. But a semantic syllabus no more replaces a structural syllabus than a structural syllabus replaces a phonological syllabus, or than a road map replaces an internal combustion engine. Structures still have to be learnt, and they have not mysteriously become easier over the last few years. Students have as much trouble as ever before in making questions with *do*, in saying *in the afternoon* but *on Tuesday afternoon*, in not saying *I see you tomorrow*, or in learning irregular verbs.

There exists a rather more sophisticated version of the 'notions/ functions are better than structures' argument, which goes as follows: 'Obviously we need both a list of notions/functions and a list of structures. The point is: which of them should we use as the organising principle of our course – as the backbone of the textbook? Traditional courses took the structural syllabus as the organising principle: each lesson concentrated on one point of grammar; texts were specially written to illustrate this point; exercises forced students to make innumerable uncontextualised sentences on the same pattern. This made for very artificial text material, and students never learnt how structures are combined into communicative exchanges. If a semantic syllabus is used as the backbone of the course, we can have natural realistic language from the start, both in the input material (suitably selected pieces of authentic text), and in the practice material (realistic communication exercises involving simulation, role-playing, etc). Instead of presenting the student with a pre-digested, ready-analysed version of the language (which he has to re-synthesise before he can communicate), we should expose him to real-life models from the outset. Special problems (such as difficult grammatical features) can be dealt with by "focusing" on them as they come up.'

This is an attractive view, and there is a lot to be said for the recommended approach. It is not, of course, intrinsically new. At intermediate and advanced levels (where courses have never been structure-based anyway), authentic input material and related communication exercises (such as discussion) have traditionally formed an important component of language teaching programmes. (This is the standard formula in French 'Second Cycle' textbooks, which are scarcely remarkable for being innovatory.) The question is whether it is feasible to apply this kind of approach in the earlier stages. When we are working with 'faux débutants', for instance, is 'focusing' an adequate solution to the problem of grammar teaching, or do these students need a more systematic presentation of the basic structures of the language? Most practising teachers are likely to opt for a relatively systematic approach; experience tends to show that, at lower levels, unmodified authentic input leads to confusion. If we analyse the language and tidy it up before presenting it to the student, it does become somewhat artificial, and he does have to 're-synthesise' it before he can use it. (We can, of course, help him with this.) But if we do not analyse the language for the student, he then has to do *both* the analysis and the re-synthesis for himself, and this may well prove very difficult for him. The texts in some of the boring old grammar-based textbooks were certainly grotesque. However, what the authors were trying to do was not necessarily totally misguided. Many of the basic structures of English *are* hard to master, and need a lot of attention. It makes quite good pedagogic sense to isolate specially difficult points, to demonstrate their use by giving numerous examples in illustrative contexts, and to do intensive practice on each point before going on to do more creative and realistic work. If teachers and course designers have generally preferred to take structures one at a time, it is not just because they were brainwashed by grammar-based descriptions of language. The main difficulties, at least in the early stages, are problems of form, not of meaning. It is not very hard to learn that *Where did you have lunch?* may be used to 'elicit factual information'. Students know about questions. They have them in their own languages. What *is* difficult for them is to cope with the unfamiliar *form* that questions take in English: to learn to say, without hesitation, *Where did you have lunch?* rather than *Where you have lunch?* or *Where you had lunch?* or *Where do you had lunch?* or *Where you was having lunch?* There are, certainly, cases where it is the use rather than the form of the structure that presents the problem (for instance, with the articles, or the present perfect tense). Even here, however, the student's main difficulty will be closely related to the specific form rather than to the whole of the semantic category ('When should I say *I saw* and when should I say *I have seen?*'), and a semantic presentation which teaches, for instance, 'ways of announcing recent events' may not help a student to focus clearly on the distinction that bothers him.

In concentrating on grammar, many traditional courses certainly neglected communicative reality. Examples of use in context were artificial; exercises were ridiculously mechanical; the 'more creative and realistic work' that was supposed to follow the drudgery did not always happen. Meaning was often neglected at the practice stage of a lesson (though not usually at the presentation and explanation stage). Such courses have also been criticised for giving the impression that there was a one-to-one relationship between form and meaning, so that students never realised, for instance, that an imperative could function as an expression of good wishes (and not just as a command); or that an interrogative could embody a request; or that an affirmative statement could act as a warning. (One imagines some curious conversations in the well-drilled classrooms of twenty years ago:

'Have a good holiday, Mr Dupont.' 'Yes, sir, of course, sir, at once, sir.'
'Have you got a light, Miss Schmidt?' 'Yes, I have, thank you.'
'Takashi, the school's on fire.' 'Yes, it is, isn't it?')

But obviously the defects of bad structure-based courses are not, in themselves, arguments for adopting semantically-based courses. To borrow an image from Johnson (1977) this is no more logical than saying 'My lawn-mower is broken, but my electric razor isn't, so I'll use my electric razor to cut the lawn.' In fact, one should probably beware of using any one syllabus as an organising principle or 'backbone' around which to organise all one's teaching. Even where grammar is concerned, it is dangerous to look for general solutions. There are some points of grammar which need to be drilled and isolated before the student can do anything interesting with them; other structures may be easier to manipulate, and can be learnt by including them directly in communicative exchanges. One really needs to be communicative at some points and structural at others. And of course, there are very many things besides grammar in a language programme.

'Faux débutants' are often regarded as being students who have learnt the forms of the language but who cannot use them; a consequence of this would appear to be that they need above all communicative practice. In fact, things are usually more complicated: 'faux débutants' are often strong on vocabulary but very weak on structure, and the reason why they cannot speak may well be that they have not really mastered enough grammar to put sentences together. A good programme for 'faux débutants' will probably contain plenty of structural work along with notional, functional, situational and topic teaching. A slice out of a typical course might contain the following sequence of activities (spread over several lessons):

1 Study and simple practice of *I would like* (affirmative, question, negative full and contracted forms; common uses).
2 Words for various kinds of food and drink.
3 Revision of *can*, with special attention to *Can I have* ...?
4 Study of model dialogue 'In the restaurant'.
5 Students create and perform their own 'restaurant' sketches.
6 Teacher talks about his family. Students listen and try to recall; ask questions.
7 Study of three easy structures used for making suggestions; practice in simple simulated problem situations.
8 Revision of numbers; telling the time; talking about ages, birthdays, prices.
9 Students bring photos of themselves when younger, and of their families, and talk about them in groups.
10 They play shops.
11 Revision test.
12 Past tense questions and short answers: study and drilling.
13 'Twenty questions' game on historical figures.

Pronunciation is handled by on-the-spot correction of bad mistakes, by five-minute bursts of systematic practice, and by lab sessions if there is a lab. Most class work is oral, but some reading is done in class, and students have 'take-home' reading material. Two or three textbooks are used from time to time.

A programme like this is very 'communicative' but there is nothing particularly new about it. Left to themselves, good teachers have always given their students a varied and balanced diet of this kind. The structuralist 'revolution' led people to teach one aspect of language (phonological and grammatical systems) in a much more efficiently organised way than before; it was unfortunate that the consequent respect for 'scientifically designed' syllabuses and teaching materials resulted in rigidity and in an impoverished treatment of non-structural areas of language. The communicative 'revolution' has now given us a much more systematic way of classifying speech acts according to their meanings and functions. This is a great step forward, but it would be a pity if, in its turn the new approach became a strait jacket. In the end, in fact, a semantic syllabus is no more a blue-print for communication, on its own, than a structural syllabus is. The syllabus may teach students how to persuade, or give factual information, or talk about time, but it cannot prepare students for the complex and unpredictable exchanges of real-life conversation, in which two people may greet, persuade, request, elicit information, give information, express moral attitudes, warn, apologise and take their leave all within thirty seconds. We do not really know very much about how people get from language lessons to language performance. Until we understand this much better, our most sensible strategy is to remain eclectic, basing our teaching on as many syllabuses as possible, incorporating semantic insights along with others, but refusing to be dominated by any one aspect of language description.

## Note

1   The word 'semantic' is here being used as Keith Johnson uses it in his introductory paper to this book. The word 'notion' refers to 'semantico-grammatical categories'.

# 3 Teaching the 'general' student

The two papers in this forum section are concerned with teaching the general student. In both, the writers confront the problem of basing such teaching on needs analyses, and both agree that this creates difficulties. Christopher Brumfit's paper looks at functional-notional approaches in the light of certain characteristics associated with the secondary school situation and with language learning at that level. His conclusion is that 'any strong functional-notional line at that level has inadequacies'. At the end of his paper he considers an approach which will develop fluency as well as accuracy in the student.

Keith Morrow's conclusions are more positively in favour of a functional-notional approach, though he too recognises the necessity for a needs analysis to go beyond a consideration of the purely 'instrumental', and to look in broader terms at the aims of language teaching. The approach which he advocates is one where very general 'macro-functions' of the language are used as the starting point for teaching. These 'macro-functions' may not be recognised as immediately relevant to the learner; but even if the language is not instrumentally 'useful', it is at least being shown and practised in relation to 'uses'.

These two papers agree, then, as to a central problem associated with teaching the general student in a communicative way. Their solutions to this problem are, however, quite different.

# CHRISTOPHER BRUMFIT

## 1  Syllabus content or classroom procedure?

At times, as I have watched the discussion of 'functional/notional' syl-labuses versus 'structural' ones, I have had a strange sense of people talking totally at cross purposes, and nowhere so greatly as when the argument is applied to language teaching in schools. If we read books of advice for teachers over the past thirty years, we find tremendous emphasis on methodological procedures which 'contextualise' and make the language 'meaningful'. We find the teacher being exhorted to give the students plenty of activity in 'lifelike' situations with suggestions about how to 'situationalise' the language material which is presented in the syllabus. Then, suddenly in the 1970s, we find that language teach-ing is being attacked for failing to specify *in its syllabuses* the ways in which language is to be *used* in the classroom. The syllabuses which used to consist of inventories of language items should now consist of inventories of language functions, or of semantic notions.

Now, it would be unfair to suggest that the change towards com-municative teaching is no more than a shift of terminology, so that what used to be thought of as methodology and the teacher's responsibility is now thought of as syllabus specification and the course designer's con-cern. Nonetheless, it is difficult to see how a teacher can contextualise and situationalise language without providing a great deal of function-ally appropriate activity and without providing students with practice in using and expressing the most important notions of the language. Some of the attacks on traditional grammatical syllabuses assume quite wrongly that the teacher's role is simply to present them in undigested form to the class. Such a view of syllabuses (whether grammatical or notional) can only result in bad teaching, for all syllabuses involve large-scale generalisations which must be made particular by each teacher for each class.

At the same time, it would be pointless for teachers to ignore the increase in understanding of how language is used in society which has emerged from studies in social psychology and sociolinguistics in recent years. Nor would it be sensible to ignore recent proposals for new forms of syllabus design simply on the grounds that the attack on traditional forms has sometimes been overstated. The basic question to ask is what, in the light of our present knowledge, is the best way of presenting material which summarises what needs to be known by students of a particular type. Such a summary may differ substantially in style from situation to situation, for different groups of learners need to know dif-ferent things for different purposes. In the secondary school, where the needs of learners are particularly difficult to predict, there is little justification for working backwards from a needs analysis. On the other hand a syllabus must have, explicitly or implicitly, some idea of what the language is being learnt for, otherwise it will not be possible for the teacher to make procedural choices in the classroom on any systematic basis at all.

## 2 Characteristics of the secondary school situation

English is rarely taught in secondary schools in the most efficient way possible. There are many reasons for this, most of them historical and administrative. Language teaching, and particularly English, is subject to many external political considerations which may justify giving access to many students but which will not justify spending enough money to make learning successful. Indeed, it is by no means unusual to find a social situation in which there is an entirely understandable political need to *offer* English in school coupled with an entirely under- standable social resistance to learning it on any large scale. The teacher cannot sort out this situation; indeed, all that can be done is to teach as efficiently as possible within the social and administrative constraints imposed. This means that the English teacher will usually require a syl- labus which can be taught to large, not very well motivated classes in not very well-equipped classrooms. Furthermore, work will not be intensive: three to five periods each on a different day of the week is normal.

There are, however, some advantages which can be set against this depressing picture, though admittedly they are advantages which depend heavily on the morale of the educational system as a whole. Students in secondary school are seen over a long period, they usually have a high degree of group cohesion which can be exploited in language work, and they are at an age when – for part of the time at least – a good teacher can obtain considerable *rapport* and exploit the resulting enthusiasm. All of this means that teachers can work for long-term goals and are not forced to cut corners or to look for short cuts all the time. Cost- effectiveness in education is difficult to define, and the quickest results are not necessarily the best in language learning.

We need to ask, then, how people learn best when faced with non- intensive, long-term exposure to English. We also need to ask how they learn best when there are no direct, short-term rewards. The answers to these two questions should help us to define the nature of the secondary school syllabus, and the two questions can be related to each other. Since the teaching is likely to be non-intensive, success will have to be measured in terms of slow accretion, rather than rapid results. However, there is no reason why a careful breakdown of elements in the course should not lead to success being apparent, stage by stage over a long period, providing the motivation of students is maintained from lesson to lesson. Effective communicative strategies provide one major way of maintaining motivation.

## 3  Language learning at secondary school level

Although we can say less with certainty about language learning than we like to pretend, a few generalisations are possible. First, in most situations, learning will be effective providing that there is extensive exposure to the target language and plenty of opportunities for the learner to use it. Second, in learning languages, as in learning other abilities, students tend to systematise: they create systems which may or may not be entirely appropriate, and experiment with them, and they learn by doing this. Third, they are more likely to learn if they are being encouraged by such factors as a warm and positive classroom environment, previous success in English (which implies that a course should be organised so that it appears to the students to be easy rather than difficult), and confidence in the teacher. Let us consider each of these in turn.

Recent developments in syllabus design have tended to emphasise more the limitation than the extension of language exposure. However, it is clear that the contemporary interest in authentic materials, whether spoken or written, allows the possibility of a much more extensive repertoire of materials for the teacher to expose students to. Materials, whether fully or merely semi-authentic, can be used successfully if there is some structure into which to fit them. The problem comes with the model which is generally followed over production by the students. Traditionally in the foreign language classroom students have been encouraged to produce more or less what they have been taught. However, if we are to allow for the really large-scale exposure which is now possible, we also need to allow considerable opportunities for students to exercise themselves in fluency work which will encourage them to experiment with what they have heard or read. That is, we want students to develop their own transitional dialect of English as naturally as the classroom situation permits, by being given material to communicate with, and opportunities to communicate; but the material they communicate with need not – indeed it cannot – be simply what has been formally taught. It must include material which has been picked up unconsciously, from any source whatsoever, and stored and retrieved unconsciously also. In other words, the development of fluency implies that students must do many things which are not entirely predictable, which may well sound rather odd, but which will indicate that their natural language learning capabilities are being exercised and encouraged.

Such an attempt to provide fluency activity may allow students to create their own systems, and it may be promoted most successfully in a warm and friendly atmosphere, but will it not undermine confidence in the teacher, who will apparently be failing to correct when he should correct, and will it not lead to students feeling that they are not succeeding as they flounder in inadequate English? These – very serious – questions can, I feel, be answered, but answering them involves making some definite criticisms of any strong functional-notional line at secondary school level.

## 4 The basis for a secondary school syllabus

Whatever the official justification for teaching English in schools, the teacher, to be successful, must give students enough of a grounding for them to be able to continue autonomously. This means both that they should have a grounding in the basic elements of the language and enough experience of language learning to have developed their own strategies for self-improvement. Ultimately (and leaving aside problems of definition of terms and of differing student needs) students will need to be accurate, operationally accurate, for their communicative purposes. Now, since we know that all normal human beings *can* learn languages and dialects sufficiently for their purposes, our problem is not so much giving students something they have not got as enabling them to exercise latent abilities which they may have been undervaluing. Clearly the language teacher has to feed *something* in, but equally clearly it is what the student learns to *do* with that something which is more important than the fact of possession. Simplifying somewhat, what the teacher feeds in is a model of accuracy, and what the student does is to acquire fluency based on the accurate model. But note that fluency does not at once incorporate accuracy. The student must be allowed to grope, to play around with the language, to internalise it by using it, and in using it to make mistakes. However the syllabus is organised, then, and whether the aims of the course involve mainly speaking or mainly reading and writing, the teacher will have to offer some opportunities for work which is aimed at accuracy, and other opportunities for work aimed at fluency. Important as the accuracy work may be, it will be during the fluency sessions – whether silent reading, or group discussions of various kinds – that the strategies for independent learning, and indeed the real internalisation of the language, will be being developed.

This means that the syllabus must make possible opportunities for both accuracy and fluency work. The fluency activities will involve a concern with the message rather than the form of the message, and will of course have to be carefully graded according to the level of the class. However, even from very early stages, students can be asked to reconstruct dialogues which they have only been exposed to once, so that they cannot *remember* them, they can only *recreate* similar messages, or shout out in English the actions which are being mimed to tell a story. And nearly all language exercises in textbooks can be discussed in groups, even with very inadequate English, from an early stage, if the teacher encourages sufficiently. The success of such an approach depends mainly on the teacher explaining fully what is involved in language learning, so that students are aware that at times they are developing fluency and will not be corrected, while at other times they can have all the formal correction they need, when accuracy is being sought. Eventually, of course, students will be fluent enough to be able to correct themselves without losing the message, but at the early stages the ability simply to maintain communication at all costs is needed. From this will develop confidence, and once such confidence is established the problems of fault-finding can be coped with.

If students can be persuaded, then, that at certain times in English work they are concentrating on being accurate, and at other times on being fluent, they will be able to accept the difference between traditional assumptions and this style of teaching. However, such a style takes us a long way from the standard functional-notional syllabus, for it emphasises the process rather than the ends of the process. The syllabus itself may be specified in grammatical terms; the situations used by the teaching materials may systematically incorporate any notional or functional categories thought appropriate for the particular group of learners, but the basis of the syllabus will not be functional or notional in the normally accepted sense.

The syllabus will be specified grammatically, because syntax is the only generative system so far described for language, and – since time is at a premium – a generative system will be more economical as a way of organising language work for student learning than a non-generative taxonomy of items (such as a list of functions is at the moment bound to be), or a random selection of items, unsystematically collected. However, any attempt to contextualise or situationalise the grammatical items will involve a variety of language functions being used and a variety of notions being realised. It will not be difficult to bargain appropriate functions or notions (if they appear to be unduly neglected or omitted altogether) against the syntactic forms being used. That is, the ordering of items in the syllabus will be determined by a cross-fertilisation between functional and grammatical categories, but with the generative system fundamental. You could thus conceive of the syllabus as a grammatical ladder with a functional-notional spiral around it:

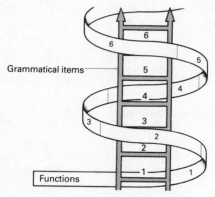

But this syllabus model, however neat it may look, has not in itself overcome the objections to the grammatical syllabus which David Wilkins has outlined in several places,[1] for those are essentially objections to a static view of the dynamic process of language learning and use. Nor does the standard notional syllabus overcome these objections. An emphasis on the processes in the classroom does help in this direction, however, for the raising of fluency to a position equal to that of accuracy forces teachers to allow learners to develop their own interactive abilities, to create their own mini-linguistic-communities, and therefore to function interactively with others, using English as best they can. On its own, this could lead to a fluent classroom pidgin. But coupled with a heavy input of more or less realistic materials, both spoken and written, together with systematically organised work on accuracy, the learner will have been given a chance to develop and use acquisition abilities which are all too rarely exploited at the moment in most classrooms.

Such a procedure as has just been outlined exploits the main advantages of the secondary school system. It allows students to develop and mature while providing constant activity with English; it exploits the group coherence which is characteristic of classes in secondary schools; and it enables the teacher to be both systematic and flexible in approaching the needs of classes and individuals. It allows, above all, the communicative process to be centred where it belongs, in the people learning to use the language and not in the static listings of the syllabus designer.

## Note

1 See particularly Wilkins (1976).

# KEITH MORROW

One of the most interesting spin-offs from the ideas behind notional syllabuses has been the way they have encouraged us to look carefully at the reasons·why learners are in fact learning a foreign language. In part this is due to the inherent characteristics of an approach which sets out to teach people how to express meanings; you have to choose what meanings you are going to teach.

A grammatical syllabus does not have to face up to this problem because the rules of grammatical structure can be exemplified without regard to the use which is being made of the structure to convey meaning. Furthermore, since these rules are finite in number it is possible to see the job of language learning for *all* learners as being that of learning them.

Being forced to choose meanings presents both opportunities and problems. The opportunity is to design a programme which appeals to the learners immediately through its clear relevance to their needs in using the foreign language; the problem is to design such a programme when the needs of the learners may not be easily specified or may be extremely varied. This problem is the central one for those attempting to develop notional syllabuses for the 'general' learner. In this paper I want to look at two possible solutions.

But first I want to suggest that the term 'general' learner is itself misleading. It conceals within itself a number of different types of learner, whose problems and expectations will be very different. Consider the following variables:

1  *Language background of the learner*. Similarity between native/ target languages.
2  *Length and type of foreign language learning experience*
   a)  Past
   b)  Prospective
3  *Amount and type of contact with speakers of the target language* (and indeed of any foreign language)
   a)  Past
   b)  Present
   c)  Prospective
4  *Attitude towards study of the target language* (and indeed any foreign language)
   a)  Among family
   b)  Among peers
   c)  Among wider language community
5  *Personal characteristics of the learner*, e.g.
   a)  Age
   b)  General level of educational attainment
   c)  Personality type

The answers we get to the questions implicit in these variables seem to me at least as important in determining the content of a language teaching programme as is the question of 'purpose'. In other words I am suggesting that a clear division between those learning a language for some specific (often vocational) purpose, and 'general' learners is over-simple. All learners bring to the task of learning individual characteristics, some of which they may share with a wider group, some of which they may not. The important problem for a teacher is to avoid stereotyping students on the basis of a superficial analysis. ESP courses often suffer on this account because the assumed commonality of purpose is allowed to outweigh other differences which may, in fact, be more important. Courses taught to students whose reasons for learning the language may be heterogeneous or unspecified (sometimes called TENOR – Teaching English for No Obvious Reason) are at least in the position of avoiding this pitfall. But how might such courses operate on the level of selection of content, given the lack of an Obvious Reason?

The first solution to this problem, with which I want to deal fairly briefly, is that suggested by the Council of Europe team and is the one implicit in the design of *The Threshold Level* (van Ek: 1975). Borrowing their terminology, we may call it the solution of the 'common-core'. The rationale behind this solution is that if you look hard enough, it is possible to identify certain uses of language which will be common to all learners of a foreign language (or more specifically, in the case of *The Threshold Level*, to all Western European learners of another Western European language). Thus *The Threshold Level* sets out certain categories of communicative function, certain topics, certain roles, certain notions (and even in an appendix certain grammatical forms derived from these) which, it is argued, provide a specification of a minimum competence in the foreign language – for any member of the very wide target audience.

The basis of the selection of the items which occur in *The Threshold Level* is what might be termed 'instrumental' need. It represents the author's view of the uses a learner might actually make of a foreign language for general tourist and social purposes.

As such it is clearly attractive as a basis for syllabus design for students who can relate their language learning to these instrumental needs. For an 'adult' learning the language in order to visit the foreign country on business or for pleasure it seems in this respect ideal. But what instrumental need does a 13 year old in Lancashire perceive for learning German? What of the Italian child in 'scuola media'? Why is he learning English?

Stretching the concept of instrumental need to fit such situations seems to me to rob it of much of its potential value elsewhere. And furthermore, insisting (even by implication) that language learning at school level must be purely instrumental in nature seems to me fundamentally misguided on broader educational grounds. Does this mean then that we must abandon the idea of needs-oriented teaching of the uses of foreign languages at school level?

No. But it does mean that we must re-define the notion of 'need' and must break out of the mental straitjacket imposed by the over-enthusiastic adoption of narrowly-perceived 'relevance' as the final arbiter of content. This, in essence, is the second solution to the problem of the 'general' learner and I want to consider it in more detail.

The sorts of needs which may be catered for in learning a foreign language in a school context are many and varied, and in most cases will extend far beyond the instrumental. At various times foreign language learning has been seen primarily as a mental or intellectual exercise, a means of broadening general cultural horizons through acquaintance with foreign literature or civilisation, or a means of social advancement. Only the last of these corresponds in any sense to the 'instrumental' need discussed above, and none of the explicitness which characterises modern needs analyses is attached to it. This is not the place to discuss the merits or de-merits of any of these answers to the question, 'Why are the pupils in this class learning English?' The point is merely to illustrate that there is the possibility of more than the answer, 'So that they can ask a policeman the way when they visit London.' Asking the question, though, is important, for the answers we get must shape our teaching programme not only directly, but also in relation to the rest of the curriculum. Equally, the answers we get must be communicated to the pupils. The most important consequence of achieving an answer – or set of answers – is that teachers and pupils have a reason for their activity and an end in view. The most soul-destroying approach to teaching or learning a foreign language is to do it merely because it is timetabled, without any attempt to relate it to some goal. As I suggest in my other paper in this collection, the psychological motivation of working towards some agreed and useful end is one of the most important benefits that pupils and teachers can expect from the ideas about language teaching and learning discussed in this book. Agreeing on what is 'useful' in their own context is perhaps the first job the pupils and the teacher have to do; and structuring the teaching/learning process so that each part of it clearly relates to the goal they have established is perhaps the most important task the teacher faces.

I am thus suggesting that a wider view of 'useful' than simply short-term, immediate instrumental need may often be appropriate. But at the same time I do not want to give the impression that there is no chance of making 'general' language teaching relevant to practical ends. What is necessary is to consider these ends in terms of higher order goals than is commonly done at present.

In many functionally oriented textbooks and syllabuses available at present the basic unit of organisation is taken as an individual category of communicative function. Thus we find units dealing with e.g. 'apologising', 'asking for permission' or 'greeting'. An organisation such as this clearly implies for the learner that the main point of what he is to learn is the function involved. Where such functions relate very clearly to a perceived instrumental need, this is probably an advantage – for the motivational reasons outlined earlier. But where instrumental needs cannot be easily identified, such an overt relationship between target behaviour and unit focus is perhaps unfortunate. Offering such a clear and low-level objective may invite its rejection as being irrelevant by a 'general' learner. If the objective is pitched at a higher level, though, such an immediate criticism may be forestalled.

In *Notional Syllabuses: Theory into Practice* (Wilkins: 1976), David Wilkins describes how in some materials developed at the Centre for Applied Language Studies at the University of Reading,[1] the decision was made to give certain teaching units 'macro' labels such as 'making arrangements', 'making plans' or 'socialising'. For Wilkins, perhaps the most important characteristic of units bearing such labels is that they encourage the chaining together of individual functions in an interactive way – interactive between the functions themselves and between the participants in the conversation. Equally important, though, is the fact that such units allow the introduction of a wide (and variable) amount of language within a context of authentic language use. Functions, notions and topics may be introduced but these individual elements may cease in this context to be the immediate end of the lesson itself. Rather, where necessary, they can be considered as exemplifications on the basis of which more general conclusions can be drawn about the way the language works.

This apparently subtle shift of emphasis is nonetheless extremely important. In any situation where a practical end is foreseen it is rather difficult for a learner to refute the suggestion that e.g. learning to social- ise is a relevant objective – it would on this level be equivalent to claiming that learning the present perfect was irrelevant. But it has this important difference. Learning to socialise is learning to do something – it provides the opportunity for learning the language in use. What language is learnt may be specified differently for different sets of general learners, and will certainly be different in terms of notions, individual functions, complexity of discourse and grammatical forms at different stages of the overall syllabus. But at any stage, these individual elements may be considered either in their own right or, alternatively, as building blocks out of which a general – and generalisable – chunk of language in use is created. The key word here is 'generalisable'. Working in this larger scale means that whatever language is presented to the students can be considered not only in terms of its own 'practical' value, but as a jumping off point for exploration of other parts of the system. In this way, new language of almost any sort can be introduced, related to the main theme and practised, with coherence being given by this inter-connection backwards and forwards. Coverage of a wide range of language is thus possible. Where the learner recognises it as being relevant in its own terms then he can take advantage of this; where such relevance is not perceived then the language is treated as exemplificatory. But always it springs from, and can be brought back to, an instance of use. The approach is thus clearly differentiated from one which presents instances of language – in individual formal or functional categories – in self-contained units merely for their own sake.

There are of course problems. As Wilkins (op. cit.) points out, an immediate one is to find enough 'high-level', interactional categories to provide a springboard for the wide coverage of language necessary. It would be difficult to base a five-year secondary school syllabus on just the three given here. The second problem is motivational. Can the interest of the learners be maintained in a programme which concerns itself with a relatively few 'macro-functions'? This is in fact a problem capable of empirical investigation and can perhaps be tackled by the ingenuity of course designers and teachers; but it is a problem nonetheless.

The advantages seem to me, though, to outweigh these problems. Providing a basis for illustrating or constructing the language in use in some systematic way seems an essential pre-requisite for teaching students how language operates above the level of form. A model such as the one discussed here offers something for even the most general of learners.

## Note

1   The materials referred to here are an early version of *Communicate*, which after much subsequent re-writing has been published as Morrow and Johnson (1979).

# Part B: Methods

# Introduction

## KEITH MORROW   Principles of communicative methodology

One of the most striking characteristics of English language teaching in the UK in the past few years has been its pre-occupation with language rather than teaching. We have recently been interested much more in *what* should be taught than in *how*. With few exceptions[1] research workers and course writers have focussed their attention on the content of the language programme rather than the ways in which this content should be taught. Notional syllabuses are widely debated and discussed; communicative methodology is still largely unexplored.

This may seem to some a rather sweeping claim. After all, it might be argued, activities such as role-play are now much used. What are they if not communicative? The answer of course is that role-play may or may not be communicative, but it is in itself merely an isolated activity. A consistent methodology is more than just a collection of activities or techniques. It requires an underlying set of principles in the light of which specific procedures, activities or techniques can be evaluated, related and applied.

A number of terms have been introduced in the preceding paragraph which it is perhaps worth clarifying briefly. By *method* I mean some overall means of achieving the general objectives of a course; a method will be realised as the carrying out of a set of procedures or activities, procedures or activities which will have been chosen by the teacher because they together relate coherently to the way in which it is hoped to reach the course objectives. A method is thus realised as a set of *procedures*; the procedures themselves involve the use of specific *techniques* to ensure their success. In an ideal language course it should therefore be possible to see a set of precise objectives in terms of which the classroom procedures, and the techniques which the teacher uses to implement them, have been structured and applied. My feeling is that thus far little communicative language teaching has been 'ideal' in these terms. Too often it has concentrated on a specific technique (e.g. dividing the students into groups or pairs) or procedures (e.g. role-play); too rarely has there been much evidence of an overall method.

The aim of this paper is, then, to consider some of the principles which might guide us in our search for a method. It will not be concerned with particular procedures – they will be mentioned in other papers in this section. But the principles considered here should certainly suggest criteria by which teachers can judge procedures proposed to them, which they can take into account in developing their own, and which they can use to relate specific procedures to each other and to the overall aims of their teaching.

Before discussing what a communicative method may be, let us clarify immediately one thing which it is not. It will be noted that earlier a distinction was drawn between *notional* syllabuses and *communicative* methodology. This distinction is crucial. The mere adoption of a notional (or, more specifically, functional) syllabus does not guarantee that we are going to teach our students to communicate. Functions are expressed through elements of the language system; in other words a functional course is ultimately concerned with language forms – just as a grammatically-based course is. The difference may lie simply in the way the forms are organised. But communication involves much more than simply a knowledge of forms; it depends crucially on the ability to use forms in appropriate ways. The problem with most first-generation 'functional' textbooks is that they have concentrated too much on setting out forms – not enough on practising communication. That is why it seems to me that this distinction of terminology is so important. In this paper we are making no assumptions about the form, content or even existence of a syllabus; we are interested in ideas that might help us to see that our students can use the language they learn in order to communicate, without concerning ourselves with the way in which this language is specified.

## 1  Principle one: Know what you are doing

I mean by this that the focus of every lesson (or part of a lesson) should be the performing of some operation – learning how to do something. Of course this is not a sufficient clarification because 'something' could be chanting verb conjugations or reciting Shakespeare. In fact I mean that the starting point (and end point) of every lesson should be an operation of some kind which the student might actually want to perform in the foreign language. In reading, this might be understanding a set of instructions; in writing it might be a letter reserving accommodation at a hotel; in listening it might be a weather forecast on the radio; in speaking it might be asking for directions in a strange city. All these operations can be approached on a variety of different levels of sophistication, and bearing them in mind throughout the teaching/learning process ensures that there is a clear answer to the student who asks, 'Why am I learning this? What am I learning to do?' Learning the question form of the 3rd person singular of the present tense because it is on page 23 of the textbook is one thing; learning it so that you can ask questions at a railway station ('Does this train go to Birmingham?' 'Does it stop at Reading?' etc) is quite another. Every lesson should end with the learner being able to see clearly that he can do something which he could not do at the beginning – and that the 'something' is communicatively useful.

In some respects, the change that is needed here is largely a psychological one. Very mundane and prosaic activities such as pattern drilling can be given a communicative dimension if teachers and students ask themselves why they are doing them and are able to relate them to the performance of some communicative task. At the same time, this principle must be equally clearly borne in mind when doing activities which seem more overtly oriented towards communication. Role-play, for example, can only be communicative to the extent that the students (and the teacher) see it as contributing to the performance of some real and specific task in the foreign language. Otherwise it, too, can become merely empty mouthing.

## 2 Principle two: The whole is more than the sum of the parts

One of the most significant features of communication is that it is a dynamic and developing phenomenon. In other words it cannot easily be analysed into component features without its nature being destroyed in the process. It is of course possible to identify various formal features of the way langauge is used communicatively and these can be studied individually. But the ability to handle these elements in isolation is no indication of ability to communicate. What is needed is the ability to deal with strings of sentences and ideas and in the oral modes (speaking and listening) these strings must be processed in what is called 'real' time. When you are having a conversation with somebody you cannot study what they say at length before producing an appropriate reply; the whole process must be instantaneous. It goes without saying that many users of a foreign language find this extremely difficult and their communicative ability is thus severely hampered. In the written modes, the time pressure may not be so severe but it is still not enough to be able to decipher or produce individual elements of the message. What is needed is the ability to work in the context of the whole.

Thus a crucial feature of a communicative method will be that it operates with stretches of language above the sentence level, and operates with real language in real situations. Interestingly, this principle may lead to procedures which are themselves either synthetic or analytic. A synthetic procedure would involve students in learning forms individually and then practising how to combine them; an analytic procedure would introduce complete interactions of texts and focus for learning purposes on the way these are constructed. Some discussions of the differences between 'analytic' and 'synthetic' approaches to language teaching[2] have obscured the fact that both of these may be made to share the same concern with the 'whole' rather than the 'parts'. A communicative method is likely to make use of both.

## 3  Principle three: The processes are as important as the forms

A method which aims to develop the ability of students to communicate
in a foreign language will aim to replicate as far as possible the processes of communication, so that practice of the forms of the target language can take place within a communicative framework. I would like
to look at three such processes which can be isolated and which can be
incorporated either individually or together in teaching procedures.
Without denying the value for certain purposes of exercises which
incorporate none of the following, the general point may be made that
the more of them that are incorporated, the more the exercise is likely
to be communicative rather than mechanical.

### 3.1  Information gap

In real life, communication takes place between two (or more) people,
one of whom knows something that is unknown to the other(s). The
purpose of the communication is to bridge this information gap.[3]

This may seem to some a gross over-simplification of the uses of language. What about comments such as 'Hello' or 'Nice day, isn't it?'
Surely no transfer of information is taking place here. In fact it depends
on what you mean by 'information'. Communication is taking place
here, but the information which is transferred is of the 'interpersonal'
(social) type rather than the 'ideational' (factual).[4] In other words, the
speakers are exchanging or confirming information about their social
relationship.

In classroom terms, an information gap exercise means that one student must be in a position to tell another something that the second student does not already know. If two students are looking at a picture of a
street scene and one says to the other, 'Where is the dog?' when he
knows that the dog is sitting outside the post-office because he can see
it as clearly as his fellow-student can then this is not communicative.
There is no information-gap. But if one student has the picture of the
street scene and the other has a similar picture with some features missing which he must find out from the first student, then the same question becomes real, meaningful – and communicative.

This concept of information gap seems to be one of the most fundamental in the whole area of communicative teaching. Any exercise or
procedure which claims to engage the students in communication should
be considered in the light of it, and one of the main jobs for the teacher
can be seen as setting up situations where information gaps exist and
motivating the students to bridge them in appropriate ways.

### 3.2  Choice

Another crucial characteristic of communication is that the participants
have choice, both in terms of what they will say and, more particularly,
how they will say it. From the point of view of the speaker this means

that he must choose not only what ideas he wants to express at a given moment, but also what linguistic forms are appropriate to express them. Deciding on these under the severe time pressure which language use involves is one of the main problems which foreign users of a language face and is an aspect of communicative ability which has been frequently overlooked hitherto in the classroom. A similar problem confronts the listener.[5] The choice which is open for the speaker means that there is always doubt in the listener's mind about what is to come next. This means that an exercise where speaker and listener are controlled in their language use by the teacher fails to practise this aspect of communication.

### 3.3 Feedback

The third and final process of communication that I want to discuss is to some extent implicit in the two already outlined. When two speakers take part in an interaction, there is normally an aim of some kind in their minds. This is what I referred to earlier as the operation or task which might form the basis of a classroom activity; successful completion of the task is the aim the participants have in mind. In real life, one person speaks to another because he wishes, e.g. to invite him, to complain to him, to threaten him or to reassure him and this aim will be in his mind all the time he is speaking. What he says to the other person will be designed to reach that aim, and what the other person says to him will be evaluated in terms of that aim. In other words, what you say to somebody depends not only on what he has just said to you (though this is obviously very important) but also on what you want to get out of the conversation. The strategies and tactics involved in using language in this way are of fundamental importance in communication, and again they are left out of account in a method which fails to give practice in using language for real purposes.

Taken together the three processes outlined above seem central to the development of any procedure for teaching the communicative use of language. If students are to practise this in the classroom then the activities in which they engage must take account of them. It is a moot point[6] whether procedures which do not incorporate these processes are automatically without value – but they are certainly not communicative.

### 4 Principle four: To learn it, do it

It is now widely accepted that education must be ultimately concerned not just with teaching but with learning. One consequence of this is that what happens in the classroom must involve the learner and must be judged in terms of its effects on him. Another, equally important consequence is that learning becomes to a large extent the learner's responsibility. The teacher can help, advise and teach; but only the learner can learn. Both of these ideas have direct implications for a communicative method of language teaching.

We have seen how developing control of the use of language involves the student in doing things, in making choices, evaluating feedback, bridging information gaps. Such activities demand an environment where doing things is possible. Sitting in regimented rows under the eagle eye of a magisterial teacher, addressing all remarks to or through the teacher – this is a scene which destroys all hope of communication. There are problems of course, particularly at secondary school level, in combining activity with discipline, but a cardinal tenet of learning theory is that you learn to do by doing. Only by practising communicative activities can we learn to communicate.

However, the above should not lead us to conclude that the teacher can just sit back and let the students get on with it. There is still a great value in a framework within which learning can be structured, and the provision of this framework is largely the responsibility of the teacher. The differences between a lesson organised around e.g. a grammatical structure, focussing on form and one organised around the idea of learning to 'do' something in the language will be considerable, but the essential point is that both can – and to my mind should – be organised. There is no reason why a communicative method should not encompass stages of presentation, practice and production, the ideas behind which are perhaps more familiar in a grammatical context.[7] *What* is presented, practised and produced will be quite different, as will the ways in which it is done, but the principle of organisation seems to me as relevant and valid here as it was before. Much published material which claims to be communicative turns out to be effective at only one of the three stages, and the extent to which it embodies a total method is thus rather limited.

## 5 Principle five: Mistakes are not always a mistake

One of the most frequently voiced criticisms of a communicative approach to language teaching is that it encourages students to make mistakes, particularly of grammar. There are probably two factors which may account for this and they should be viewed rather differently.

The first possibility is that the student may be taught by a teacher who believes that 'trivial' mistakes of grammar or pronunciation do not matter as long as the student gets his message across. The second is that the student may be forced into activities for which he has not been prepared, and in an effort to deal with them he makes mistakes. The attitude one takes to these two possibilities must depend on the context in which one is working, but two points are worth making in general. Firstly 'trivial' mistakes of grammar or pronunciation are often not trivial at all. Even a teacher who adopts a totally communicative stance must accept that grammatical and phonological mistakes hamper communication, and enough of them – especially in the wrong place – can totally destroy it. Secondly, a learner who makes mistakes because he is trying to do something he has not been told or shown how to do, or which he has not yet mastered, is not really making a mistake at all. Trying to express something you are not quite sure how to say is a vital feature of using a foreign language, for few learners ever reach the stage of total fluency and accuracy in every situation, and it is often necessary to 'make do' with whatever resources one can muster. Niggling criticism of what he produces will ultimately destroy the learner's confidence in his ability to use the language.

If these two comments seem somewhat contradictory, then it is perhaps because they are. What I am trying to say is that the question of what constitutes a mistake and how the teacher should react to it is far more complex than many have so far thought. Conventional language teaching methods aim at eradicating mistakes by tightly controlling what the learner is allowed to say. When we remove these controls and encourage the learner actually to start using the language with all that this involves, then from a certain point of view problems are bound to arise; but these problems are not solved by an approach which insists on formal accuracy at the expense of use. A communicative approach certainly does not provide an easy solution to the problem of mistakes, but it at least highlights an area which some have treated over-simply hitherto; a communicative method must go back to first principles in deciding how it will reach its aim of developing the communicative ability of the student. It may well be that it will require the flexibility to treat different things as 'mistakes' at different stages in the learning process.[7]

To conclude this introductory paper let us consider briefly the place of the ideas which have been discussed in it within language teaching as a whole. Despite the concentration here on aspects of the use of language, I do not wish to leave the impression that I consider form to be unimportant in language teaching. Communicating involves using appropriate forms in appropriate ways, and the use of inappropriate or inaccurate forms militates against communication even when it does not totally prevent it. The acquisition of forms is therefore a central part of language learning; those of us interested in communicative approaches must not forget this in our enthusiasm to add the communicative dimension. It therefore follows that the principles discussed in this paper may not underlie the totality of language teaching procedures, and that a total method for language teaching may have a component which uses a quite different set of principles to teach language forms and which thus gives rise to procedures which, though not communicative, are justified in their own terms.

This view implies the rather large assumption that it is possible (and desirable) to divide language teaching into two phases – learning the forms and then learning to use them. While I think it is undeniable that language learning does involve these two aspects and that it is possible to separate them logically, it seems to me that one of the major unresolved issues in communicative language teaching is to work out under what conditions it may be more efficient to teach the forms through the uses, when a more efficient solution would be to attach uses to pre-specified and pre-taught inventory of forms, or finally, whether it is actually possible to marry the two in some satisfactory way for teaching purposes. This may seem to be primarily a matter of syllabus design, but in fact it is central to *how* we teach as well for it affects crucially the way we view the language and the activities we practise. For the moment I would just emphasise that, notwithstanding everything written here about the importance of 'use', it is possible and may in certain cases and contexts be legitimate to ignore 'communication' altogether and focus on the forms of the language. In a narrow sense, this perhaps represents a reactionary view; more responsibly, I feel it merely emphasises the need for teachers to assess their own priorities in their own situation. Finding ways to reconcile these two aspects of language in the classroom represents the biggest challenge for our profession in the 1980s.

## Notes

1  For one of the exceptions to this, see Allwright (1976).

2  For further discussion of this distinction, see Wilkins (1976).

3  I would like to acknowledge the help of Keith Johnson. I owe much of my insight into these processes and their relevance in this context to discussions with him.

4  For discussion of these 'macro-functions' of language, see Halliday (1973).

5  The use of the terms 'speaker' and 'listener' is over-restrictive here. As Ronald White points out in his paper, similar processes apply to the writer and reader of a text.

6  The point is considered further in the final section of this paper.

7  This point is taken up and illustrated in Roger Scott's paper, which follows.

# 1 The 'four skills' in communicative language teaching

The papers in this section look at some of the ways in which what we do in the classroom can reflect the ideas and principles set out in the introduction to this Part of the book.

For convenience, we have looked at each of the four conventional 'skill' areas in turn, although one of the points developed by all the contributors is that language is rarely used in one mode at a time. Indeed, one of the main effects of a communicative approach to language teaching may be the abolition in the classroom of these traditional distinctions.

The first paper, by Roger Scott, looks at some of the implications of a communicative approach to the teaching of oral production. Taking as his starting point the characteristics of oral communication outlined in the Introduction, he shows how these may fail to be developed in a structural approach to language teaching and suggests ways in which a 'communicative' lesson may take account of them. Three key elements (*stating objectives, contextualisation* and *practice and transfer*) are identified and the writer discusses differences between what needs to happen in order to practise communication on the one hand and what often happens in language teaching classrooms on the other. He discusses the particularly important issue of what constitutes a 'mistake' in learning terms. Despite uncertainty about the place of communicative ideas in an overall teaching method, the author is quite unequivocal that to ignore this aspect of language learning is simply to mislead the student about what using a foreign language involves.

The theme of oral communication is developed by Marion Geddes in the second paper. This time, though, the emphasis is on listening rather than speaking, i.e. on the language user as the recipient rather than the producer of messages. For this writer, the key element in a communicative approach to 'listening' is the purpose which underlies it. 'What is important to note is that . . . we never listen without a purpose.' Examples of the sort of purpose we may have in listening are given and the point is made that listening often overlaps with other areas of language use (e.g. listening and speaking; listening and writing). The author then considers the classroom implications of the above, dealing in turn with the selection and presentation of texts and the sorts of listening tasks which may be set. The paper concludes with practical examples of such tasks, which are discussed and evaluated.

Ronald V White's paper, the third in this section, develops in relation to reading many of the points made in the preceding paper. The overlap between the two receptive areas of listening and reading is clearly considerable and many points of similarity are established and discussed, e.g. the idea of purpose, and the importance of devising classroom activities which teach rather than simply test. In this paper the author contrasts what he terms a 'pedagogical' approach to the teaching of reading with a 'communication' approach, pointing out the ways in which the latter relates to the general communicative principles established in the Introduction. Examples are given of reading tasks which the student might be set, and these are followed through to see how reading may become one step in a sequence of communicative activities. To conclude, the author considers reading in relation to writing and shows how the idea of a 'dialogue' between writer and reader (and vice versa) can help the student to gain an insight into the workings of the written language.

Keith Johnson also touches on the question of integration of skills and considers how sequences of activities which involve writing can be built up. One of his considerations is how sequences of activities can stimulate the imagination in preparation for free writing tasks where the student is asked to write an essay on some abstract topic.

The writer also argues that because pieces of written work can be taken home by the teacher and studied at leisure, they are often subjected to far more scrutiny than students' spoken language. This often results in too much attention being paid to structural errors. The paper considers ways in which the focus of attention in both the production and assessment of written work can be placed on the 'conveying of information' rather than on structural correctness.

In the final section of his paper, Keith Johnson considers writing at the paragraph level. He takes up a point made in the introduction to this section, that a communicative method emphasises operation at levels above the sentence. It is for this reason, he argues, that the most interesting recent work in the teaching of writing has dealt with the paragraph level. He suggests a number of techniques for focusing attention on paragraph structure, and for developing the skills of cohesion and coherence. Many of the techniques he discusses involve a large element of what we would traditionally call reading comprehension, and like Ronald White, he emphasises the interrelationship between the reading and writing skills.

The last paper in this section, by Donn Byrne, deals specifically with the topic of integration alluded to in several earlier papers. The writer begins by contrasting the role of integration in a communicative approach with its role in a more traditional approach. In this latter case, he argues, integration usually means reinforcement. Language introduced and practised in one skill area (often speaking) is reinforced through practice in another (often writing). In a communicative approach, on the other hand, integration is a means of providing natural contexts for language use. Sometimes the contexts will call for speaking, sometimes for writing, sometimes for combinations of 'skills'. The 'skills' used depend upon the activities involved and the paper shows how activities, as well as individual skills, can be developed into an integrated sequence.

# ROGER SCOTT   Speaking

In the Introuction to this Part of the book oral communication is typ-
ified as an activity involving two (or more) people in which the participants are both hearers and speakers having to react to what they hear
and make their contributions at high speed. Each participant has an
intention or set of intentions – goals that he wants to achieve in the
interaction. Each participant has to be able to interpret what is said to
him, which he cannot predict exactly either in terms of form or in terms
of meaning, and reply with what language he has at his disposal in a
way that takes account of what has just been said and which reflects his
own intentions at this point in the interaction.

It is sometimes said that a structural approach, when it is orally
based, with plenty of classroom activity, succeeds in doing this. It does
not. It is important not to confuse plenty of student talk with learning to
communicate. They are not synonymous. A communicative approach to
speaking emphasises the use of language above the level of the sentence. Structural approaches, on the other hand, are concerned with the
production of grammatically accurate sentences. Whilst it would be foolish to deny the value of a structural framework as perhaps the only
means of arriving at a systematic understanding of how words are permitted to combine at the level of the sentence, it is equally foolish to
assert that a structural approach can provide students with rules for use,
no matter how active the method. The kind of activity that goes on
inside a classroom where the structural approach is being used is
confined to the appraisal of utterances on structural criteria and in isolation from each other. Students learn question forms. They learn to
negate statements, they learn imperatives and they learn conditionals.
They learn how phrasal verbs behave. They learn passives, subordinate
clauses, deletion, cleft sentences, and so on. But what question a cleft
sentence is an appropriate answer to, or how to make the right choice of
form to express appropriately a given function in a given situation is not
touched upon. Certainly dialogues are used, but their purpose is not to
teach rules of communication, appropriacy or use. No matter how many
grammatical forms may appear in a structural dialogue, the focus is
always a structural one and no account is offered of how a sentence
takes on meaning from its relation to surrounding utterances and non-
linguistic factors. No attention is paid to who is speaking. (Speakers are
frequently labelled simply 'A' and 'B'.) There is no clear reason for the
dialogue to have occurred, except as an opportunity to give frequent
examples of the target structure(s). Structural dialogues lack communicative intent and you cannot identify what *communicative operations* the learner can engage in as a result of practice. The result of
purely structural practice is the ability to produce a range of usages, but

not the ability to use forms appropriately.[1] This is true even in cases where it looks as though communication is being taught. For example, the exclamation form, 'What a lovely day!' might be covered. But the interest is in the form, not on when and where to use it or what you achieve by using it.

A lesson using a structural approach can thus be a very active lesson, and be successful in promoting grammatical accuracy. However, a close look at what goes on in the classroom will reveal that these activities are not related to practising communication. Either the teacher or a student says something that is designed to produce a response of a certain grammatical form from another student. Frequently a question and answer technique may be used. The teacher either asks a question himself, or directs another student to do so, and another student answers. The questions are often about a text that is being studied and the language used is so-called 'reporting' language. Each utterance exists in isolation. There is no relationship between one utterance and the next, so that in the end the student can manipulate a form in isolation, but he has not had any experience of using it in relation to other utterances. Furthermore, because the language is reporting language, the learner never gets experience of doing language. The learner learns to say, 'He apologised for being late' but never learns how 'he' actually apologised, and therefore may never find out how to apologise at all, let alone how apologies may be realised appropriately in different ways as circumstances vary. In performance terms, this results in students who over-use reporting verbs when they find themselves in real communicative situations. Thus you hear students saying, 'I suggest' or 'I promise' instead of 'Why don't you . . .?' or 'I'll do it' which are more appropriate in the circumstances.

The communicative approach on the other hand makes sure that the interactions which take place in the classroom are replications of, or necessary prerequisites for, a communicative operation. The focus changes from the accurate production of isolated utterances to the fluent selection of appropriate utterances in communication. The learner is now concerned with using language, not English usages. In order to do this, learners take on roles and interacts with other learners who also have roles. What they say is determined by the role they have, their communicative intentions and the contribution of the other learners. The range of communicative models (two, three or more people involved) will reflect the learners' needs. The role of the teacher changes, too. Instead of being the person who provides prompts that trigger utterances of a certain structure from the students, the teacher now sets up the conditions for communication to take place. Hence, the teacher will actually assume roles to model the language for the learners, or act as someone for the learners to communicate with. The teacher also has to be able to set up the conditions for students to practise communicative operations themselves.

There is nothing particularly mysterious about the process of teaching speaking on a communicative basis. It consists of the same stages as learning any language skill:

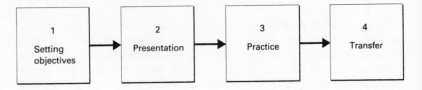

Only, in the case of teaching for communication, there is a difference in type of language item and the type of activities. So we may have the following:

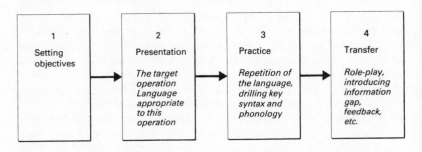

Here the presentation phase presents a whole language operation in context, from which the students or the teacher may take out the key items. In the practice phase, these are drilled and the main features of syntax and phonology are focussed on. The transfer phase consists of putting to use the language items in situations that are analogous to that of the presentation phase. For this role-plays and games are the chief strategies, and it is here, perhaps, that the biggest difference exists between a structural and a communicative methodology. The difference is not only one of strategy, although the strategy is crucial as a means of achieving the objective. There is also the difference of criteria on which success is judged. As the objective is successful communication, how well this takes place is not a function of grammatical accuracy alone. Indeed it is possible for successful communication to occur with a poor command of syntax. Syntax is only one of several related aspects of performance that contribute to communication. To take an example: suppose you are working with beginner students. You have detected a need on their part – they often want to ask for things. A good, neutral way of doing this is to use the form 'Could I have . . .?' As soon as you add what is being asked for, you encounter the problem of definite and indefinite articles and also the use of 'some'. Now the question is whether this matters. I do not think it does. The crucial aspect of performance is whether the student uses an appropriate form to ask for things. Hence, if a student says 'Could I have spoon, please?', gets it and says 'Thank you', with reasonable intonation, communication has been successful. It does not matter *at this stage* whether the articles and 'some' are handled correctly.[2]

It is more important to have a crack at using the right form and intonation. This is a justified view, but it has led communicative teaching to be accused of paying too little attention to grammatical accuracy. The charge is unfair, and neglects the relevance and effect of other considerations which come into play when language is being used to communicate. It might well be argued that grammatical accuracy has received too much attention hitherto and that too little attention has been given to rules for use.

It now remains to look in more detail at some of the strategies needed for teaching speaking in a communicative way.

## 1 Stating your objectives

In the case of teaching speaking communicatively, the teacher's job is to put across what operation the students are going to learn. This can be as simple as telling the students that the lesson is on asking for and giving advice. Just tell them. For a fairly abstract operation such as giving advice, an approach of this kind may be the best. But there are many operations, and therefore many ways of conveying objectives. For one such as apologising and forgiving, it may be possible to *show* what the objective is by showing the students a cartoon strip, for example, that depicts somebody spilling coffee over someone in a cafe. In this case you invite the students to try to say what would be said in the circumstances.[3]

In this way you make clear what is to be learnt, and, assuming the students do not know what to say – if they do, teach something else – they now know they have a learning problem. (They must also *need* to know the language, of course.) Another approach is to use the cartoon strip with speech balloons which convey the whole learning load to the student, just at a glance.[4] In practice, a combination of illustration, problem setting and explanation may be used to make one's objectives clear. Telling the students explicitly what they are going to learn has been criticised as involving too much reliance on metalanguage, but this is far more defensible than the structural equivalent: saying, for example, that they are going to learn the present continous tense. 'Giving advice', for example, is something that anyone can grasp the meaning of, with the use of a dictionary if necessary. The cartoon methods have the virtue of carrying a good deal of contextual information as well as indicating what is to be learnt. It provides the link, so important in communicative teaching, between the language used and the culture. Consideration of visual means of making your objectives clear leads one naturally to a consideration of contextualisation in a communicative context.

## 2  Contextualisation

Contextualisation is the means by which the meaning of a language item is made clear. Structural approaches used two broad categories of contextualisation to do this – one unsuccessful, the other successful. The unsuccessful one puts the item in a context but does not incorporate into the context any details that really clarify the meaning of the item. For example, the item is put in a story and used over and over again, so that students become familiar with the form, but not with the idea it expresses. The more successful type of contextualisation exemplifies the new item and, by means of clues in the context, demonstrates what it means. Whatever type of contextualisation is used in a structural approach, however, the concern is to convey the ideational content of the form, not its use. To contextualise communicatively, however, you have to do more than convey this level of meaning. Indeed, from a communicative point of view, an item only takes on meaning as a result of the total context in which it is used and an item without context in this sense cannot properly be said to have meaning at all. It must therefore be made clear to the students, as a general observation about how language works, that what you say takes on its meaning as a result of the context, where context is taken to mean a constellation of factors, such as who the speakers are, their relationship to one another, what they are trying to do, what has just been said, where they are, and so on, in addition to the ideational content of what they are saying. Hence, a question form ('Is that your coat on the floor?') may be an order (to pick it up), or 'I beg your pardon' may be an indication that you are insulted or offended. A form may function in various ways, and the meaning of a 'sentence' may change according to the way it is said and when.

If students have been informed about, and convinced of, the importance of (a) learning communicative operations, and (b) the effect on meaning of the constellation of factors alluded to above, then they can be expected to appreciate and look out for information of this kind. Such information may already have been given to the students at the stage when objectives were set, if, for example, cartoons or other visuals were used. If this has not been done, then the students have to know who the language they are going to learn is appropriate for and under what conditions. So language is contextualised in terms of who is speaking to whom, where and why.

## 3 Practice and transfer

The presentation of the material is followed by drilling. Because we are concerned with teaching communicative operations and not with structures *per se*, two drilling procedures commonly used in structural teaching are no longer appropriate. The first is the use of question and answer to practise the language presented. This is appropriate only for the practice of 'reporting' language. It is not a procedure that works for teaching 'doing' language. In this communicative context any questions asked after the language is presented are to check whether students have understood what is going on. The answers are not judged from the point of view of grammatical accuracy, but on whether they indicate students have understood who the people are and what they are trying to do. Similarly, a second technique, pattern drilling, is often not relevant. Where, for example, part of the target language is 'So do I' to indicate agreement with someone's statements of what they like, it would be irrelevant to drill 'So does he', 'So do they' and so on, because, although they are formally related, they are not functionally related. 'So does he' is not an agreement and is therefore not relevant to learning the operation in hand (Agreeing). Communicative teaching aims to build up sets of language items for a given function, not formal paradigms *per se*.

It is a feature of communicative methodology that practice follows quickly upon presentation. It may start with choral repetition by the students of the language presented and then move into individual responses directed by the teacher. The teacher can ask students to repeat a line and give the answer himself. He can then ask individual students to ask the questions and prompt individual answers. When he is sure that students are competent (not necessarily perfect – see above) in handling the language, he can put the students into pairs and ask them to practise the dialogues with each member of the pair taking it in turns to perform the two roles and make appropriate substitutions. It can be seen that, even with material and operations as simple as these, some amount of information gap can be introduced. Student A may decide e.g. what he is going to ask about, but Student B does not know until he is asked. Furthermore, there is also an element of feedback, because what Student B can say may be determined by what Student A asks. Note that this differs radically and importantly from the popular kind of dialogue in which each student of a pair can choose the next line from a set of given possibilities which will 'make sense' regardless of what the other student has said. In such material, there is no information gap and no allowance for the effects of feedback.

Elements of information gap and feedback can be increased by some very simple means, beyond suggesting 'prompts' from which a free choice can be made by the learners. The 'conversation grid' below illustrates a means of offering great freedom, while at the same time making clear to the learner the 'moves' that are open to him during practice. In this case the particular exponents chosen by each speaker are not laid down, but the plan is kept to. The precise content, course and outcome of the conversation can be determined and influenced by either speaker. In this particular case, learners have just practised asking where something is (outdoors in a town) and giving directions. One student has a list of places he/she wants to find and another has a map of a town.[5]

**Practice**
Have conversations like the ones below.

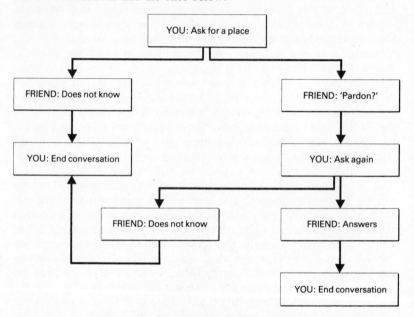

Note here that the whole operation is being taught and practised. How a student answers the questions affects the outcome of the conversation in terms of what it is appropriate to say. This aspect of feedback is catered for in 'End conversation' on the grid, because students have to discriminate between what they say if they are helped and what they say if they are not. Clearly this material is intended for pair practice, but could also be used with the teacher taking one part. This activity, using conversation grids, can be adapted for use with groups of three or more.

The application of the procedure described above is not confined to beginner or elementary level. Any interaction that is composed of a limited number of easily defined 'moves' may be practised in this way. However, this technique cannot be applied to sustained and extended practice, where even the wide limits set by conversation grids would inhibit the learner's freedom too much. Accordingly, the communicative approach emphasises the importance of games and role-plays as a way of setting limits to activity that are sufficiently well-defined, yet also sufficiently wide, to promote practice in using language freely over longer periods of time. These procedures are discussed in papers later in this book.

In this paper I have tried to show how the communicative approach to teaching speaking can be organised to teach whole operations. It has to provide input in the form of language appropriate for the operation, carefully contextualised with regard to the roles of the speakers, their attitudes, ages and intentions. Practice takes the form of rapid transfer to further applications of the target operation, thereby putting language to use as soon as possible. Role-plays and games are important because they present learners with the opportunity to practise speaking under conditions that are as close as possible to those of normal communication, involving information gap, choice and feedback. The criterion for success is how well the learner can perform the target operations, responding to information gap and feedback, given the language he or she has at his disposal. From a communicative point of view, using language well is not a simple question of grammaticality, but one of overall appropriacy and acceptability.

How far instruction can proceed entirely on communicative lines is a matter of intense debate. But one thing appears certain: it is only by using language under the conditions which a communicative approach tries to create and in the way this approach advocates that one can develop, as a learner, one's ability to use language outside the institution where it is being learnt. Any approach which does not recognise the insights of the communicative approach and incorporate them into instruction misrepresents to the learner what the ultimate task in learning a language is.

## Notes

1   This distinction between *usage* and *use* is taken from Widdowson (1978).

2   This is an illustration of the point made in Principle 5 of the first paper in this part of the book. The idea that at different stages of the teaching/learning process we may consider different things as 'mistakes' is an important one.

3   A textbook which makes use of this is Johnson and Morrow (1979).

4   This is used in Scott and Arnold (1978) and Arnold and Harmer (1979).

5   This example is taken from Scott and Arnold (1978).

# MARION GEDDES   Listening

Communication is by definition a two-sided process: a message cannot be communicated unless there is someone to receive it. Discussions of the implications of a communicative approach to the teaching of spoken language tend to emphasise the development of the student's ability as sender of spoken messages. In this paper, by looking at the language activity normally called listening, I want to focus on the development of the student's ability as receiver of spoken messages. Obviously he will need to have some knowledge of the language forms he hears. What I am particularly interested in, however, is how we can train him to understand and respond to the realisation of these forms in communication.

It is of course somewhat misleading to suggest that, when discussing spoken communication, we can isolate listening from other language skills. There *are* times when the only language skill we use is listening, as when we eavesdrop on a conversation on the bus, or listen to the radio or attend a public lecture. But, more often than not, other language skills will be involved in the communication. With so much of our lives spent in conversation with others, listening and speaking are the two that most often co-occur. This means that the on-going speech reflects and requires the feedback given by the addressee(s), and a process of mutual adjustment is evident as the roles of addressor and addressee are continually exchanged. The implications for a teaching methodology are clear: often we cannot restrict our focus to speaking *or* listening but must consider both skills together.

Reading and writing skills may also be needed at the same time as listening skills. I said above that we may sometimes only listen to a lecture. But a college or university student will probably want to take notes as well as listen, both to help his concentration as well as for later recall purposes. For some lectures he may need to use reading skills to follow a printed handout or notes written on the blackboard. Examples can be found in social communication as well. When a friend phones me to suggest we spend the evening at the cinema together I may continue to listen to him talking about arrangements for meeting as I skim through the newspaper to find out what time the film we want to see starts.

The nature of the additional skills required will depend on our purpose in listening. What is important to note is that, as in reading, we never listen without a purpose. Even when we are not the intended receivers of a communication, as in eavesdropping situations, we listen with a purpose – either because we are spies or because we have nothing better to do on a tedious bus journey or because our curiosity has been aroused and we wish to satisfy it. And our purpose in listening will affect how we listen and what we select from the stream of sound. Again, this has obvious implications for a teaching methodology.

The more one tries to analyse just what the listener's task involves, the more impressed one becomes at the human ability to understand speech! Widdowson (1978, Chapter 3) has made a useful distinction between 'hearing' and 'listening'. He uses 'hearing' to refer to the listener's ability to recognise language elements in the stream of sound and, through his knowledge of the phonological and grammatical systems of the language, to relate these elements to each other in clauses and sentences and to understand the meaning of these sentences. He reserves 'listening' to refer to the ability to understand how a particular sentence relates to what else has been said and its function in the communication. It is at this stage that the listener selects what is relevant to his purpose and rejects what is irrelevant. This distinction is similar to Rivers' (1966 p 142) distinction between two levels of activity in a foreign language: the recognition level and the selection level. I will restrict myself to 'listening' and the selection level.

I now want to look at some of the implications for classroom methodology of the ideas outlined above. Let us start with the question of text selection. When we select listening texts for our students, we sometimes want the text to serve as a model for the students' own production. Texts of this kind are not sufficient, however, to prepare the student for all his eventual communicative needs. In selecting additional texts we will be guided by these needs and by the suitability of the texts for training the student to 'listen' and select. What does this mean in practical terms?

In considering his needs we will be concerned with such variables as the number of speakers and the sex and age of each, the kind of English they speak (native or non-native; American, British, etc; accent and dialect), register, subject matter. In addition we will want to help the student to understand spontaneous speech with all its 'ums' and 'ers', its ungrammatical features, incomplete sentences and mid-utterance changes of direction. This raises obvious problems. An authentic text of spontaneous speech may confront the student with so many problems that he will simply panic. We need to find texts that will give the student controlled and guided experience. Elsewhere, Ron White and I have described in some detail how this can be done by simulating authentic speech.[1] Essentially it involves using some form of incomplete or semi script that will help the speaker(s) control content, vocabulary and structure without inhibiting the spontaneous occurrence of features of unscripted speech. Simulated authentic speech techniques also help the materials designer to link texts with tasks that train the student in selective, communicative listening.

To take account of the student's communication needs and at the same time give him texts which give him appropriate experience implies that we should have access to a vast library of recordings. For most teachers this is not possible. But at least an appreciation of the need will encourage teachers to start building up such a collection and to locate and gain access to centralised sound libraries.

A note about radio broadcasts. These are one of the most commonly cited sources of spoken texts – and certainly it is an important one. However, when choosing radio broadcasts, remember that many are not examples of spontaneous speech. Some may be good examples of 'calculated spontaneity',[2] others may make few attempts to simulate spontaneity and be easily recognised as written discourse read aloud.

The next aspect I want to consider is text presentation and in this connection two points are important. The first relates to the medium through which the text is presented. Most teachers have access to tape recorders and many to language laboratories. These are essential aids. However, they have a major disadvantage: the voices we hear are disembodied. Unless we are listening to the radio or to someone on the telephone we interpret the speaker's message with the help of our knowledge of the meaning of gestures, facial expressions, body postures, and eye-contact. Very few cross-cultural studies of these visual paralinguistic communication features have been made and it is not clear to what extent they are a problem to students from different cultural backgrounds. But clearly, the nearer we can get to simulating the kind of communicative situations that the student will encounter outside the classroom the better. The aid that can help us most is the videotape recorder. Its presence is still the exception rather than the rule in most schools and even those schools which do have one suffer from a shortage of appropriate materials. At this stage of development it is up to materials designers and teachers with access to video equipment to share their ideas on how to best exploit its potential, bearing in mind that the addition of a visual channel of communication will affect the nature of the tasks that we use with sound-only texts. At the moment videotape recorders are not suitable for practice that requires quick and frequent replay facilities. However, current technical developments indicate that in a few years time this disadvantage will have been overcome and that videotape recorders will be as flexible in use as audiotape recorders.

The second aspect of presentation I wish to consider relates to class versus individual use of texts. So far I have avoided talking about 'teaching' listening. It seems to me that a teacher cannot teach a student to listen. He can only help him to practise and learn. The teacher can point out various important characteristics of speech which aid understanding, for example phrases that indicate how a speaker orders his information ('I'd like to make one or two points'; 'first of all'; 'by the way') or phonological features such as when a speaker drops his voice and hurries, indicating that what he is saying is less important – and that if the student did not catch his words he should not panic. It is also the teacher's job to provide the student with appropriate texts and to devise tasks that will guide his listening and integrate it with other skills, and to be on hand to help him if serious difficulties arise. The student should be given plenty of opportunities to practise listening and develop confidence in his abilities through successful practice without being interrupted by the teacher.

This can be achieved in a language laboratory, where the students may or may not all be listening to the same text and where they have individual control of their tape recorders. Even better, a listening centre can be set up in the school or college where a continually growing collection of taped material is stored (in an ideal world on both video and audio tape) and where students can come when they wish, selecting tapes according to their interests, their linguistic ability and the time available.[3]

Now let us turn to the question of listening tasks. I have said that, as in reading, we never listen without a purpose. Much of what Ron White will say in this connection in his paper on reading in this book can be applied equally well to listening. We should not ask a student to listen without identifying – or helping him to identify – a purpose that relates to the communicative value of the text. As in reading practice, we can help the student by giving him instructions or setting a task. The task should be as realistic as possible so as to help the student relate what he is doing in the classroom to something he might want to do in real life in the foreign language.

I would like to develop Keith Morrow's example[4] of listening to a weather forecast on the radio – something that a student studying in Britain might often want to do. When I listen to the weather forecast I do so with a reason. Perhaps I am planning a picnic the following day and want to know if the weather will be fine. Perhaps I am planning a longer trip and want to anticipate any bad weather that will make driving difficult or unpleasant. Perhaps I have an elderly relative living in another part of the country and I want to know how he will be affected by the weather – ice or snow making walking outside difficult and dangerous or perhaps a lovely sunny day when I can imagine him enjoying a pleasant day in a park. Sometimes I may just idly wonder what the weather at home is going to be like, without paying much attention to detail, since wind, sun or snow, I will still have to go to work!

Translating my first reason into a listening task, the following instructions could be given to a student with a tape recording of a weather forecast:

Today is 10th July. You live in London. Tomorrow you plan to visit Brighton on the south coast. Listen to the weather forecast and decide if you should take your raincoat with you to Brighton.

Notice that this task is similar to 'search reading'. The student needs to understand very little detail, but he has the problem of selecting the relevant part from the whole.

A task with a weather forecast recorded in winter might require the student to use a worksheet like the one on the next page:

## A trip to Edinburgh   Student worksheet 1

*The weather forecast*
You live in London. You are planning to drive to Edinburgh tomorrow. As it is winter and you have not done the journey before you are not sure which route to take.

1   Listen to the weather forecast and make notes on the map below about weather that could affect your trip.
2   Decide which is the best route to take.

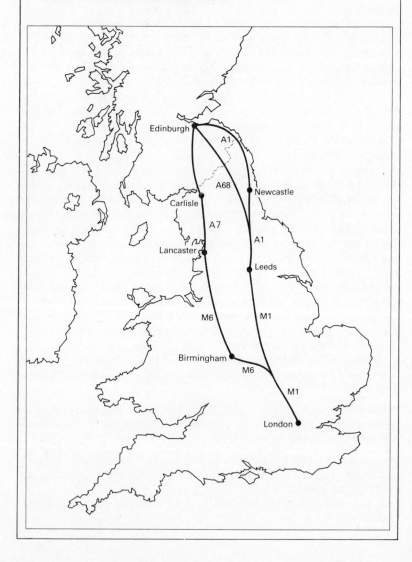

The map provides the student, who is probably not familiar with the geography of Britain, with the mental map that the British motorist might have. The task requires the student to select what is relevant for him in the role he has been given (someone who lives in London and is driving to Edinburgh tomorrow). He then has to interpret the explicit message given to him by the weather forecaster to elicit its implicit message for him and decide which route he should take to Edinburgh.

Very often of course a real life decision-making process is not as simple. In this example there may be factors additional to weather conditions that could affect his choice of route: major roadworks causing long delays on a particular road; hilly country that makes a route that appears short on the map slow to drive on. A second listening exercise might be a taped telephone conversation (authentic or simulated) to the Automobile Association providing this information, with instructions to the student to find out which is the fastest route to Edinburgh. A third exercise could be another conversation, this time with someone who is already familiar with one of the routes and recommends it for its scenic value.

In real life, the gathering of this information might be shared by three different people, perhaps travelling together to Edinburgh. This suggests that in the classroom we might use a jigsaw listening technique[5] and divide the class into three groups, each group listening to only one of the three texts. Their purpose in listening is extended. They now have not only to select information but also to be able to share it with others who have not heard it. After listening, the students will be regrouped, making sure that at least one member from each listening group is in each discussion group. The students will share the information they have gathered and use it to come to a decision as to which is the best route to follow. Here we have moved to a much broader integration of skills and communicative practice.

I said earlier that speaking very often co-occurs with listening. One way of giving the student some fairly controlled practice in this co-occurrence is through well contextualised language laboratory· exercises where the student will either have to listen carefully in order to know how to respond to the speaker on the tape, or will be required to complete a task that relates to listening but is also dependent on his contribution to the interaction.[6] Some would argue that drills of this kind are not communicative because the student has no choice in how to respond. I believe that this kind of integrated listening and speaking practice should not be dismissed too lightly. An an example I offer the following language laboratory exercise, which could be an alternative to the taped dialogues I suggested above. Notice that in this particular exercise the student can speak without understanding the other speaker. However, the note-taking task requires him to understand the other speaker – which he can only do if he relates that utterance to his own.

## A trip to Edinburgh   Student worksheet 2

*Language laboratory exercise*
Imagine you are travelling to Edinburgh tomorrow by car. You have prepared a checklist of questions that you want to ask your friend, David:

1   Steep hills on the A68?
2    "    "    "   " A7?
3   Motorway restaurants between
    Leeds and Newcastle?
4   Motorway restaurants between
    Birmingham and Lancaster?
5   Petrol stations on the A1?
6    "        "      "   " A68?
7   AA garages between
    Newcastle and Edinburgh?
8   AA garages between
    Carlisle and Edinburgh?
9   Interesting places to visit
    on the A1?
10  Interesting places to visit
    on the M6?

1   Do the exercise, using the checklist to ask David questions.
2   Do the exercise again, but this time stopping your tape after each of
David's answers. Make notes beside the checklist about the information he
has given you.

## Language laboratory exercise: A trip to Edinburgh

A  When did you get back from Edinburgh, David?

B  Last Wednesday. You know, I'm sick and tired of that journey. I've had to do it so many times now.

A  Well, you're probably the best person I know to tell me about the different routes to Edinburgh.

B  Certainly. What do you want to know?

NOW LOOK AT THE CHECKLIST ON YOUR WORKSHEET AND LISTEN TO THESE EXAMPLES.

1  B  I know all the routes to Scotland very well indeed.
   A  *I see. And do you know if there are any steep hills on the A68?*
   B  Yes, lots. It goes up and down all the time! But it's a quiet road on the other hand. Not much traffic.

2  A  *I see. And what about the A7?*
   B  That's a much better road. A bit more traffic on it though.

3  A  *I see. And do you know if there are any motorway restaurants between Leeds and Newcastle?*
   B  Well, that's not all motorway of course. It's really the A1. But you should be able to find places to eat.

4  A  *I see. And what about between Birmingham and Lancaster?*
   B  No problem. There must be two or three at least.

NOW YOU PLAY THE PART OF THE WOMAN. ASK DAVID FOR INFORMATION. USE THE CHECKLIST TO HELP YOU. (repeat 1–4.)

5  A  *I see. And do you know if there are any petrol stations on the A1?*
   B  No need to worry about that. Lots.

6  A  *I see. And what about on the A68?*
   B  Again, no problem – as long as you're not travelling on a Sunday. There's so little traffic on that road on Sundays that most of them are closed.

7  A  *I see. And do you know if there are any AA garages between Newcastle and Edinburgh?*
   B  Yes, there are quite a few. They're listed in the AA handbook.

8  A  *I see. And what about between Carlisle and Edinburgh?*
   B  Same applies. You'll find them in the AA handbook.

9  A  *And are there any interesting places to visit on the A1?*
   B  Well, just after crossing the border into Scotland, there are some beautiful places on the coast.

10  A  *I see. And what about on the M6?*
   B  The M6 goes along the edge of the Lake District. If you've never been there before, it's well worth a stop. You could even break the journey and spend the night there.
   A  That's a good idea. I hadn't thought of that. Yes, I must think it over. Thanks.
   B  Well, I hope you have a good trip. Bon voyage!

Communicative listening tasks can thus engage the student in a wide variety of activities, often requiring him to use other skills, both verbal and non-verbal, aural and graphic. Whatever the tasks, they will at least approximate authenticity in language, context and communicative purpose, thus helping to train the student for communication outside the classroom.

## Notes

1   See Geddes and White (1978).

2   This is the title of a radio broadcast given by John Hilton, a popular pre-war broadcaster, in 1937. It is printed in Sutherland (1953) pp 399–404 and makes interesting reading for any language teacher interested in recording materials.

3   The listening centre that has been set up at the University of Nancy, France is described in Riley and Zoppis (1976).
For practical advice on how to set up and organise a centre, see Kerr and Leisching.

4   Given in the first paper in this part of the book.

5   For further examples of jigsaw listening exercises for intermediate students, see Geddes and Sturtridge (1979).

6   See for example the drills in Ahrens (1977).

# RONALD V WHITE   Reading

Some prophets have suggested that the ability to read and write is becoming increasingly less important in our age of spoken and visual communication. However, new developments in printing technology married to the rapidly developing field of telecommunications mean that we are entering an era in which we will have access to a world-wide library of printed materials, available in the form of print-outs or video displays to virtually everyone. Significantly, these new developments will assume a literate audience, and so the skills of interpreting information presented in printed form will continue to be important in the new age being ushered in with the advent of the silicon chip and micro-processors.

Unfortunately, such technological innovation surpasses our knowledge of the reading process derived from research, and we still know very little about how people learn to read, even though we do know somewhat more about what it is that a skilled reader is able to do. Furthermore, most of the investigations into reading – both acquisition and performance – have focussed on the reader reading his own native language. Consequently, when it comes to considering the non-native language reader, we are even further from having an adequate understanding of the reading process than we are with the native language reader.

Yet, even though we are unable to provide satisfactory answers to such a fundamental question as 'How do we learn to read?', we are now concerned with finding answers to another important question, i.e. 'Why do we read?'

One obvious answer is that we read in order to obtain information which is presented in written form, but the nature of the information so obtained requires more explicit definition. By 'information' I mean content which is cognitive (or intellectual), referential (or factual) or affective (or emotional). So, then, the first answer we can give to our question of why we read is that we read *referential* material in order to obtain factual information with which to operate on our environment, e.g. a set of instructions on how to use a piece of equipment. Secondly, and overlapping with the first purpose, we read material whose content is *intellectual* rather than factual as a way of augmenting or developing our own intellectual skills so that we can more effectively manipulate ideas, possibly with the aim of influencing the behaviour of others or of determining the outcome of a series of operations, e.g. making proposals for a project. Thirdly, we read for *emotional* gratification or spiritual enlightenment, i.e. for pleasure or self improvement.

These reasons for reading are essentially practical. That is to say, reading is carried out for a purpose other than reading the language itself. Just as we read messages in order to be able to do something else, so too the student who is learning a foreign language (and who is reading in it) should be less concerned with the language than with the messages it is used to communicate. That is, his interest will be in use rather than usage, with function rather than form.[1] He wishes to *do* something with language other than simply learn it.

Hitherto, conventional approaches to the teaching of reading have tended to obscure the fact that we read for different purposes and that different kinds of skills are involved according to the reading task. On the one hand, the 'explication de texte' approach has emphasised detailed textual study and slow, careful reading with more or less equal attention being given to each item regardless of its status in the overall structure and organisation of the text. On the other hand, the speed reading approach has advocated developing a very fast reading rate both as an end in itself and as a way of increasing comprehension. Furthermore, advocates of speed reading have tended to imply that only the fast reader is an effective and efficient reader.

It is fairly clear, however, that purposive reading is not simply a case of either reading very painstakingly or reading very quickly, and that developing purposive reading skills in the student will involve training him to adopt a number of different reading styles related to his reasons for reading. In fact, it is the ability to switch styles according to purpose which makes for efficient reading, and the trend in current practice is towards developing reading techniques which Pugh (1978, pp 53–55) has termed *scanning* (to locate a known item), *search reading* (for information), *skimming* (to gain an idea of the organisation of the text), *receptive reading* (to discover accurately what the writer wishes to convey), and *responsive reading* (to reflect upon what the writer has written). Lunzer and Gardner (1979) recognise essentially the same styles of reading, and they conclude that 'in searching for ways and means of improving reading comprehension it would appear that a prime consideration should be the involvement of pupils in their reading. At the heart of the matter is the willingness to reflect.'

Clearly, receptive, responsive and reflective reading require an active involvement on the part of the reader and, while the efficient reader will undoubtedly switch styles with little or no conscious thought, the apprentice reader will need to be given overt instruction in developing the strategies involved, even though it has to be admitted that very little is known about the actual processes involved in these different reading styles or strategies. One approach to overt teaching of reading is what we might call the pedagogical approach, by which I mean the teaching of reading for its own sake with little or no attention being given to reading as part of a process of communication. A second approach, which I will call the communication approach, sets reading firmly in the context of the communicative use of language.

In what I have called the pedagogical approach, the student will be given a reading text accompanied by a selection of questions. These may be open-ended, closed or multiple choice. They will tend to focus on elements unique to the text in question, and the information gained by answering the questions will be unrelated to any task outside of that performed in completing the answers to the questions. Although the student may well develop useful, transferable reading strategies from undertaking such tasks, any such pay-off is likely to be coincidental because students 'rapidly learn to treat comprehension exercises for what they are: irrelevant chores that one must complete to satisfy someone else. There is little transfer to reading in subject areas.' (Lunzer and Gardner, *op. cit.*) Furthermore, the approach as I have characterised it tends to focus on an extremely limited type of 'comprehension' based on sentence-level reference. Finally, much emphasis is given to testing the students comprehension while giving him no real help in developing whatever skills may be needed in order to read efficiently or comprehend effectively.

In the communication approach to reading, on the other hand, the student is first of all given a reason for reading. The most cogent reason for wanting to read anything is that the writer conveys – or is expected to convey – something which will be of use to the reader ('use' here being defined to include utilitarian as well as affective purposes). This means that the reader will read because what he gets out of the text will fill an information gap, and only by reading a given text is that gap likely to be filled. Notice that I say 'likely' because, of course, in developing efficient reading, two of the strategies which the reader has to acquire are those of scanning and search reading. Learning to reject the irrelevant is as important in this context as dealing effectively with sources of information which are relevant to the reader's purpose.

Having given our hypothetical student a reason for reading, we may now give him some instructions as to how he should go about the reading task, and this will depend on the type of reading style we wish him to develop. For instance, we might specify a task such as the following.

You have been asked by some friends from your country to book a four day coach tour for them for the Easter weekend. There are six of them, and they wish to visit some places of scenic beauty and cultural significance. They can afford up to £70.00 each.

a) Read the texts which describe a number of different tours.
b) Make a list of four suitable tours.
c) Write a letter to the tour operator or operators to find if there are any places available on the tours concerned.

The reading material supplied to the student can be either a selection of tour brochures, or simply one brochure in which a variety of tours is described. The student's first task is to identify only those tours which conform to the requirements stated in the rubric, viz. period: four days, time: Easter weekend, cost: up to £70.00, places: scenic and of cultural significance. The student could be instructed to scan the texts to identify only those tours which took place at the Easter weekend. Next, he could be told to scan again to identify those tours which fall within the price

range specified. Thirdly, he could search read for detailed information
on places visited on the tours. Finally, he could transfer the relevant
information to some other form, such as a table summary. The table
could be supplied as part of the exercise, or it could be devised by the
student himself. Either way it might look something like this.

| Name of Operator | Tour Number | Cost | Places Visited |
|---|---|---|---|
|  |  |  |  |

This table summary could then be used as the basis for group or class
discussion before the student writes the letter or letters specified in the
final part of the rubric.

In this exercise, the information gathered from the reading activities
became input to speaking or writing activities. A similar principle is followed in jig-saw reading, following a technique very effectively employed by Marion Geddes and Gill Sturtridge (1979) in their material on
jig-saw listening. In an exercise based on this procedure, information
required for the completion of a target task is distributed among two or
more sources (talks or dialogues in the case of listening comprehension,
reading passages in the case of reading comprehension). These sources
are then made available to individuals or sub-groups within a class such
that each sub-group will obtain only some of the information required
for the target task. Following acquisition of this information, the sub-
groups exchange their information so that information gaps are filled
and the target task (which may be a discussion or a written composition)
is completed.

Exercises of which these are examples incorporate three important
characteristics as compared with the traditional pedagogical exercise discussed earlier. Firstly, the student is given a reason for reading, often in
the form of a problem which has to be solved. In solving the problem,
the student reader is doing something with language. Secondly, the
reading task may involve translating information in the text from verbal
to visual form. This type of activity, called transcoding, links language
to other forms of communication.

Transcoding is a two-way process, since it can involve not only the
translating of verbal to visual, but of visual to verbal as well. Thirdly,
the problem-solving and transcoding activities based on the reading task
provide for the integration of the four skills. Reading becomes one step
in a sequence of activities involving listening, speaking and writing and
the exchange of information. Such integration of the four skills may
serve to demonstrate to the student that, as Keith Morrow has noted in
the first paper in this Part, writer and reader communicate with each
other in the same sort of way as speaker and listener.

The parallel between spoken and written communication may be more obvious if we consider some characteristics of the process of writing. The writer, unlike the speaker, is not in a position to receive immediate feedback from his audience; but he may imagine himself into the role of audience, and this is not difficult because, of course, the act of writing involves the act of reading as well. For instance, as I write (and rewrite) this paper, I read back over what I have already written so that what I write next will tie in with what precedes it. In doing this, my reading self questions my writing self about the formulation of the discourse.

It may be helpful to the apprentice reader if he is made aware of the dialogue implicit in writing – especially in discussion or argument. The reader's role in the dialogue is to formulate questions to which the writer's statements are responses. The written text then becomes part of an interaction between writer and reader, with the reader contributing actively towards the creation of the discourse. This concept of reader as participant in a joint act of creation is not a particularly recent innovation. As undergraduates twenty years ago, my fellow students and I were introduced to the principle of the active reader when our psychology professor urged us to apply the SQ3R sequence in our reading as proposed by Robinson (1946): Survey, Question, Read, Recite, Review. The second step in the sequence is Question, and what the reader is supposed to do is to formulate questions to which the writer responds. In other words, the reader and writer participate in a silent dialogue.

The view of reading as a conversation between the writer and reader leads to another feature of reading which is shared with spoken interaction, viz. that the listener/reader can finish what the speaker/writer is going to say in advance of his saying it. In other words, the reader (like the listener) is able to predict what will come next. Our ability to predict depends on several factors. Firstly, there is our knowledge of the code and of the fact that certain combinations of items are more likely to occur than others. Secondly, there is our knowledge of the topic. Finally, there is our knowledge of the relationship between what is being communicated and the real world.

It appears that the skilled reader in his native language is able to use this knowledge, which he has acquired through his experience of learning and using the language, to trade-off the various cues to meaning – lexical, syntactic, rhetorical – as a way of comprehending a written text as efficiently as possible. Unfortunately, the foreign language learner is still in the process of acquiring this knowledge, and it is not clear whether explicit training in guessing ahead and using contextual and other clues to meaning will actually help the foreign language reader to read any more efficiently. It may well be that such training will make the student more aware of what is involved in reading as a skilled activity and that this will make him more sophisticated as a reader, more adaptable in his approach to reading, and more tolerant of the uncertainties which he must face when reading in a foreign language.

From the teacher's point of view, one of the main difficulties lies in the provision of suitable reading exercises aimed at promoting predictive reading and the maximizing of contextual and extra-textual clues to meaning. One technique involves a variation on the multiple choice procedure, in which the text is laid out so that at various nodal points a range of possible completions is provided. The reader has to use his understanding of the text to select the most appropriate continuation from those offered, his choice receiving confirmation or otherwise from the section of the text which follows the selection provided.

Clearly, in being required to make conscious decisions as to the form or content of the text during the reading process, the student is becoming actively involved in the construction of the text and in the creation of a piece of discourse. This active contribution is, of course, in line with the view, already discussed, that reading is a joint act of creation on the part of writer and reader. This approach can be extended in exercises which involve the explicit construction of a passage following a specification given in note or visual form. For instance, the student can be provided with headings which specify types of function, this list forming the rhetorical organisation of the text. The student then has to match a scrambled set of sentences with the specification to produce the finished text. Much the same kind of procedure can be followed with longer texts, in which scrambled paragraphs are matched to a flow diagram or other visual representation of the structure of the text.

By now it will be clear that we have moved from receptive reading exercises to activities which are half way to productive writing exercises. Such blurring of the divisions between reception and production owes much to the now widely held view that both reading and listening involve a much greater active contribution by the receiver than was traditionally accepted. It also follows the trend towards integration of the so-called skills of reading, writing, listening and speaking, which in itself is a feature of many interpretations of communicative methodology, with its emphasis on the transfer of information from source to receiver. And it is through this transfer of information that the reader is given a motive for reading, listening, speaking or writing, since each activity is instrumental in enabling the student to perform a task beyond that which he is carrying out at the moment. It also means that the focus is not simply on learning the language, but on using it – a shift in emphasis which characterises the communicative approach in general and which, as I hope to have shown, is leading to some significant changes in the way we teach reading in the ELT classroom.[2]

## Notes

1   This distinction is taken from H G Widdowson (1978).

2   I am particularly grateful to my colleague Eddie Williams for comments on an earlier version of this paper.

# KEITH JOHNSON   Writing

## 1   The information gap and jigsaw principles

A central characteristic of communicative language teaching, mentioned in various contributions to this book, is that it focuses attention on the ability to understand and convey information content. The following reading comprehension exercise is 'communicative' to the extent that the student is being asked, not to comment on any point of grammatical structure or lexical meaning, but to extract certain pieces of information from written sources and to transfer them onto the application forms.

### Example 1[1]

In Winton there is a very good sports club which welcomes applications from overseas visitors.
Look at the two letters below and on the next page. They contain information about two people who want to join the club. Fill in application forms for these people.

```
                               29, Gosforth Close,
                                  Hamford,
                                    Nottingham,
                                      Notts.
                                        NG16 7EA

                                 1 Feb. 1979
       Dear John,

           I don't know whether you remember
       me - we met very briefly at Michael
       Everton's party last week. My name is
       Arturo Catania and I'm an Italian
       doctor. My wife told me after the
       party that you're the secretary of the
       sports club, which I'm very interested
       in joining. Could you please send me
       some information about how to apply.
       If you wish to phone me for any reason,
       my number's Hamford (0273) 51469.

              Yours sincerely,

              Arturo Catania

              Arturo Catania
```

2b, Lakeside Avenue,
Upton,
Notts. NG16 7AA

13 Jan. 1979

Dear Sir,
    I wish to become a member of the Winton
sports club, and would be grateful to recieve
details of subscription rates and other
relevant information. I am a teacher by
profession, and shall be in England for 2 years
(my nationality is French). I was born in
Paris on the 12th of January 1939.
    I look forward to hearing from you.

                    Yours faithfully,

                    *Odette Marie François*

                    (Miss) Odette Marie Francois

---

WINTON SPORTS CLUB: MEMBERSHIP APPLICATION

Surname __CATANIA_____ First Name(s) _____

Date of Birth __4·8·46__ Nationality _____ Marital Status __

Address _____

Telephone Number _____ Occupation _____

---

WINTON SPORTS CLUB: MEMBERSHIP APPLICATION

Surname _____ First Name(s) __Odette Marie_____

Date of Birth _____ Nationality _____ Marital Status __

Address _____

Telephone Number _____ Occupation _____

In the same way that communicative reading practice is concerned with the *understanding* of information content, communicative writing practice should deal with the productive equivalent of this ability: the *conveying* of information content. It is often truly said that in the past language teachers assessed student performance too little in terms of these abilities and too much in terms of grammatical correctness. This is perhaps particularly true in the teaching of writing because of the 'permanence' of the medium. The student writes on pieces of paper which the teacher takes home. There they are subjected to the kind of scrutiny which the student's spoken language rarely receives. The resulting 'sea of red ink' is often judgment on structural shortcomings rather than on the overall success or failure of the piece of writing to convey its message clearly. So perhaps particularly with written work we need always to remind ourselves that the aim of any communication is to 'get its message across' and that therefore this is the true criterion by which any communication should be judged. [2]

In Example 1 *understanding* the message was practised by asking the student to transfer information from letter to form. To practise *conveying* the message we may simply reverse this procedure, giving the student two completed forms and asking him to write the letters of application. If we wish to guide his writing and at the same time reintroduce an element of reading comprehension, here is a possible sequence:

## Example 2

Stage 1:   Students read Arturo's letter and fill in a form for him.
Stage 2:   Students are given Odette's form completed; they write a letter from her using Arturo's letter as a model.

But can we really claim that exercises like these truly involve *conveying* information? There is certainly information *transfer* (from letter to form, form to letter). But 'transferring' and 'conveying' are not quite the same because the latter includes the idea of a *receiver* – someone who does not have the information and who receives it by reading the piece of writing. [3] So if we are to practise true conveying of information in the classroom we need to find a way of simulating the real life situation: where a writer writes something for a reader who does not know that something already, and who learns it by means of the written communication. Example 3 on the next page creates this situation. The students work in pairs. Student 1 looks at the top of the page and covers the bottom half with a piece of paper. Student 2 looks at the bottom half of the page and covers the top half with a piece of paper. Student 1 writes a letter for Arturo, Student 2 for Odette. They then exchange letters and use the information they have been given to fill in the appropriate forms. As a final stage the students check that the forms have been correctly filled in. If not, this means either that the writer has failed to convey his message or that the reader has failed to understand it (or, of course, both!) The students, with the teacher's help if necessary, must decide which; and if the writer is at fault he must rewrite his letter to make the message clearer.[4, 5]

## Example 3

*Student 1*
In Winton there is a very good sports club which welcomes applications from overseas visitors.

i)   Arturo Catania applied to join this club. He wrote a letter to the club secretary who used it to fill out an application form for Arturo. Here is the form. Use it to write Arturo's letter of application.

```
WINTON SPORTS CLUB: MEMBERSHIP APPLICATION
Surname  CATANIA       First Name(s)  Arturo
Date of Birth 4.8.46  Nationality Italian    Marital Status M
Address 29, Gosforth Close, Hamford, Nottingham NG16 7EA
Telephone Number (0273) 51469   Occupation  Doctor
```

ii)   Your partner has written a letter of application from another person. Use this letter to fill in the application form from that person.

```
WINTON SPORTS CLUB: MEMBERSHIP APPLICATION
Surname_____ First Name(s) _____
Date of Birth_____ Nationality _____ Marital Status___
Address_____
Telephone Number_____ Occupation _____
```

*Student 2*
In Winton there is a very good sports club which welcomes applications from overseas visitors.

i)   Odette Francois applied to join this club. She wrote a letter to the club who used it to fill out an application form for Odette. Here is the form. Use it to write Odette's letter of application.

```
WINTON SPORTS CLUB: MEMBERSHIP APPLICATION
Surname FRANÇOIS       First Name(s) Odette Marie
Date of Birth 12/1/39  Nationality French    Marital Status S
Address 26, Lakeside Avenue, Upton, Notts, NG16 7AA
Telephone Number (0273) 63159   Occupation Teacher
```

ii) Your partner has written a letter of application from another person. Use this letter to fill in the application form from that person.

```
WINTON SPORTS CLUB: MEMBERSHIP APPLICATION

Surname_____ First Name(s)_____

Date of Birth_____ Nationality_____ Marital Status____

Address_____

Telephone Number_____ Occupation_____
```

Activity sequences like these involving information transfer can easily be built up, often simply by adapting exercises in existing textbooks (in the same way that Example 1 is adapted to become Example 3). Here is a further example which involves listening, form-filling, writing, and potentially speaking as well:

## Example 4

Stage 1:  Students work in pairs. Student 1 listens to a telephone conversation between Arturo and the club secretary: Student 2 to one between Odette and the secretary. Both use information given in the conversations to fill in application forms.

Stage 2:  Student 1 writes a letter from Arturo to the secretary confirming the details given by phone. Student 2 does the same for Odette.

Stage 3:  Students exchange letters. Student 1 must fill in a form for Odette, Student 2 for Arturo. They then check that information has been conveyed correctly.

The sequence can be extended to include oral practice by using one-part dialogues. The student hears only one side of the telephone conversation (which must contain all the information he needs to fill in the form). Then after Stage 3 students return to the telephone conversations and complete the dialogues by supplying the words of the other speaker. If recording facilities are unavailable, telephone conversations can of course be presented at Stage 1 in written form.[6]

The full potential of this type of sequence is realised when we move away from the idea of an application form. White (1979) and Johnson (1981) use information transfer from passage to a table which is then used as the basis for written work, and Byrne (1979) contains examples of maps being used in much the same way. The following instructions (from an exercise in a unit on 'describing objects') illustrate the technique in a sequence which transfers information from diagram to written work, and back to diagram:[7]

**Example 5**

'Work in pairs. Student A looks at the diagram of an Egyptian invention on page 107. Student B looks at the diagram of a Greek machine on page 105. Each write a description. Then show your description to your partner who must try to draw a diagram from it. If his diagram is wrong, make your description clearer so that the diagram is correct.'

The title of this section of the paper is 'the information gap and jigsaw principles', and it is worth making explicit exactly what part these principles play both in the techniques considered here and in the teaching of writing generally. One reason why the information gap is useful for the teaching of speaking is that it creates a condition of unexpectedness. If Student 2 does not know in advance what Student 1 will say to him, the former cannot work out his reply in advance; he is forced to formulate his responses quickly, and thereby develops fluency. Because writing does not involve rapid exchanges with another person, this element of the unexpected is less crucial. But the information gap principle is no less important in the teaching of writing, for two other reasons. The first is because it permits genuine information flow in the classroom. The students tell each other things they do not already know, and in this sense are genuinely communicating. The second reason is a consequence of the first. Because the students tell each other things they do not already know, the assessment of written work (by the student's partner in the examples above) focuses primary attention, as it should, on whether the writing succeeds in 'getting its message across'.

We create information gaps in the classroom by giving Student 1 information which we withhold from Student 2. Communication as the 'bridging of the information gap' takes place when Student 1 passes this information to Student 2. In this sequence Student 1 is a 'producer' only, and Student 2 a 'receiver' only. The 'jigsaw principle' streamlines the operation by allowing all students to be both producers and receivers. Thus we give Student 1 some information and Student 2 other information. Student 1 writes for Student 2 while Student 2 is writing for Student 1. They then exchange information to complete the 'jigsaw'. Both these principles operate in Example 3; we create the information gap by asking the students to cover parts of the page, and we create a jigsaw by getting them to exchange written work and fill in forms.[8]

## 2  Activity sequences

The examples we have so far considered involve writing as one stage in a sequence of activities. There are several reasons why activity sequences are attractive from a communicative point of view. One is that they provide integration of skills – a topic which Donn Byrne deals with at length in the next paper. Secondly, in a sequence of thematically-related activities each activity provides contextualisation for the one following it. As the sequence develops, the 'story line' becomes richer and more complex. The importance of rich contextualisation is by now well recognised and has already been discussed in this book by Roger Scott. Rich contextualisation of writing practice within an activity sequence helps to avoid the kind of written work about which, if we were asked 'who wrote this and for whom?' we could only reply 'an EFL student for an EFL teacher'.

In this section we shall consider two further attractions of the activity sequence, the first related closely to what has been said before:

## 2.1 The 'task dependency' principle[9]

Is the creation of an information gap sufficient to ensure that information will be conveyed in the classroom? The answer is 'no', and to illustrate why consider the following example related to the teaching of oral skills. Imagine that we wish to practise *asking for and giving information about train times*, and to do so we create an information gap drill in which Student 1 has some train times which Student 2 must ask for. Part of Student 2's task is a listening comprehension one, and we can only be sure he will undertake it if we ask him to utilise the information he is given in some way – even if this just involves him in writing it down. Without this requirement the danger is that he will, quite simply, not listen. He will have no motivation for doing so.

Requiring the student to utilise information obtained in the course of an exercise is the 'task dependency' principle. According to it, we create whenever possible a Task 2 which can only be done if a Task 1 has been successfully completed. Example 5 above is an illustration of this principle at work since the student can only draw the diagram (a Task 2) if his partner has written the description accurately (a Task 1).

Why is the task dependency principle important? For the teaching of receptive skills it is crucial to ensure that the listening or reading task gets done. But it is also relevant to the productive skills because it helps to foster in the student an 'accountability' for the way he uses language. A difference between classroom and real world which can never be eradicated is that the former shields the student from the consequences of his mistakes. Street directions given wrongly in the classroom lead only to teacher correction; in the real world they result in someone getting lost. Task dependencies can help to minimise this difference; the student's knowledge that someone in the class will read his letter and utilise its information content (returning with a complaint if that content is inadequate!) will affect the way he tackles his task. Similarly the student writing in Example 5 knows that he is accountable to his partner, and that his description will be assessed on how adequately it enables the production of a diagram.

Activity sequences are attractive because they breed task dependences. Through them we are able to develop Task 3s to depend on Task 2s, Task 4s dependent on Task 3s – and so on.

## 2.2 Activity sequences and free composition writing

One type of writing task which creates particular problems is the free composition on an abstract topic, like the 'generation gap' or 'women's place in society'. We may feel inclined to question the value of tasks like this, but we cannot ignore their frequent use in examinations for which the student must be prepared.

It is difficult for anyone to tackle an abstract topic without having the imagination stimulated in some way. Preparation is particularly necessary with young students, who have two types of problem. First they need help in relating the familiar and concrete situations of everyday life to the abstract topic of the title. It needs pointing out to them, for example, how the arguments between John next door (who wants to leave school and get a job) and his parents (who want him to go to university) relate to the abstract theme of the generation gap. Second, their attention needs drawing to the scope of the theme. It is not just John, but also Mary who feels she is old enough to stay out late; and Alfred the father whose grown-up children never come to visit him.

Activity sequences, which in themselves provide useful language practice, can play a central role in stimulating the imagination for writing tasks on abstract themes. Here is one possible sequence as a lead-up to an essay on the generation gap:

## Example 6[10]

Stage 1: An in-depth case study of one 'generation gap' situation (the case of John, for example, who wants to leave school). Students are given a series of activities based around this situation. They might begin by listening to a one-part dialogue in which John and his mother argue. The mother's lines are given and the task is to provide John's. This can lead to a role play of the actual argument — with perhaps John's brother also present who listens and (as a Task 2 ensuring listening takes place) reports to his friends the next day.

Stage 2: Stage 1 explores one concrete situation. Stage 2 widens the scope, covering more situations but in less detail. An 'agony column' of the type found in women's magazines can be used here. Students can be shown an imaginary agony column containing letters related to the generation gap theme. Their task is to write replies which they then compare with the replies of the imaginary columnist. Differences are discussed. The students might then be asked to imagine what other characters in these conflict situations would have said had they themselves written to the agony column.

Stage 3: The students are now led towards abstraction. A variation of jigsaw listening can be used here, based on a taped discussion about the generation gap — perhaps between a teacher, social worker and parent:

a) Students work in groups of three. All listen to the same taped discussion, but Student 1 concentrates particularly (and takes notes) on what the teacher says; Student 2 does the same for the social worker and Student 3 for the parent.

b) Students report to each other on the general standpoint of the character they have been concentrating on. Differences in the standpoints are discussed, with the students contributing opinions.

Stage 4: Planning and writing an essay entitled 'The Generation Gap'.

# 3 Paragraph level writing

Keith Morrow has already made the point that a communicative method operates with stretches of language above the sentence level, and it is certainly true that the method's most interesting applications for the teaching of writing relate to the paragraph level. All the examples we have so far discussed are intended to stimulate paragraph level writing, but in this section we look at techniques for drawing attention to and practising particular aspects of paragraph structure. Discussion will inevitably revolve around the twin concepts of *cohesion* – how we join sentences together to form 'grammatical units'; and *coherence* – how we organise our sentences to form 'sense units', a meaningful flow of ideas.[11]

It is once we begin to think about teaching aspects of paragraph structure that we realise how close the relationship between reading and writing really is. As Ronald White has already pointed out, writing skill involves the ability to be a reader – we cannot write successfully unless we know at each point how the reader will interpret our words and what he will be expecting us to say next. Indeed, the two skills are so closely related that we might speculate to what extent writing can be taught without the student ever putting pen to paper! Certainly time spent on analysing sample passages, in asking questions about their construction and how they reflect the writer's intent, is not time wasted. We may indeed be moved to claim that any communicative writing course must contain a large component of reading comprehension – of practice, that is, for the writer as reader.

Let us then begin by looking at techniques geared to draw the student's attention to aspects of passage intent and organisation. Precisely because of the close link between reading and writing, many of these techniques are neither clearly one nor the other. Certainly in many cases the end result is classroom discussion rather than the production of written work.[12]

The first set of techniques nearly all involve the student in some kind of 'speculation' about what comes before or after a given piece of language:

## Example 7

Give the students a passage and ask them to look only at the first paragraph, covering the rest with a piece of blank paper. They think about and discuss how the passage might continue, then look at the second paragraph and compare their guesses with what is actually written. Continue in this way through the passage. The student is here being asked to identify his predictions as a reader, speculate about passage organisation and how the writer signals this organisation. As an alternative, reverse the procedure with the students reading the last paragraph first and thinking about what might come before.

## Example 8

Dictate a paragraph sentence by sentence. After each sentence ask the students what they think the next sentence might contain. Then dictate it. This technique is taken from Donley (1976).

It is usually difficult to find passages or paragraphs which can be used in these ways without the student needing some guidance. This can be given by telling the student (by means of notes for example) roughly what points the passage makes, but not the order in which they are made.

## Example 9

A cloze passage. Give the students a passage in which some words (groups of words or whole sentences) have been replaced by blanks. The students must fill in the blanks. By careful choice of which words to omit we can lead the student to think very carefully about passage structure. Then give the students the completed passage; they discuss differences between their versions and the original.

These techniques are particularly useful for drawing attention to overall passage structure. We may also wish to focus on specific aspects of cohesion; to provide practice for example in recognising how words like 'he', 'this', etc. are used to *refer back* to someone or something already mentioned in the text:

## Example 10

Give the students individual sentences containing backward referring words (like 'he' or 'this'). They are asked to supply sentences coming before so as to make it clear what these words refer to.[13]

## Example 11

Give the students a passage containing many backward referring words. Get them to circle, box or underline these words indicating by an arrow what the words refer back to. This technique is suggested by Byrne (1979) and Raimes (1979).

Another highly productive technique for drawing attention to aspects of passage organisation, coherence and cohesion involves the assembling or reassembling of passages. Here are some examples:

## Example 12

Take a short passage (pieces of narrative are ideal) and write each sentence of it on a separate card. Mix the cards up and give one card to each student. The students must order the cards to make the original passage. If there are more students than cards, have more than one set of cards available with the students working in groups.[14]

As a second best, present the sentences to the students in jumbled order on one piece of paper. The students must number the sentences in the correct order. Here is an example using a passage taken directly from a reader.[15] The sentences are presented below in jumbled order:

> After a few minutes the man got out of the car and went into the phone box.
> They watched as the merchant and Mrs Perkin left the flat.
> 'This is it, Jan', said the man in the car to his friend.
> She was talking to a diamond merchant.
> 'Yes, I'll keep them here in the company's flat', replied Mrs Perkin.
> He went to the window and looked out.
> In the street he saw a red car by a public telephone.
> The merchant smiled.
> 'You won't want to lose these', he said. 'Is there a safe place for them?'
> Mrs Perkin was visiting Amsterdam on business to buy some diamonds.

Listen to the kind of discussion the students have while doing this type of exercise. It is highly detailed discussion about specific aspects of cohesion and coherence.

## Example 13

Insertion of information. First select a passage. The following is rather academic in tone, but any type can be used:[16]

Women in Britain are without doubt better off today than they used to be. At the beginning of the nineteenth century they seem to have had almost no rights at all. They could not vote, or even sign contracts. Their marriages were arranged, and they almost never worked. Today they can at least vote and choose their own husbands. Also, many more of them go out to work. But there is still much to be done, and woman's status in society is still below man's.

Then think of some points that could have been made in the passage. Present these to the students, who must decide where in the passage these points could have been made. Here are some possible instructions:

When he originally wrote the passage, the writer included the following points. Where in the passage do you think each was made?
a) In the nineteenth century women could not own property. Now they can.
b) Women in some parts of the world are no better off today than they used to be.
c) Today women can sign contracts.

Three points about this exercise type:—

1 It involves grasp of passage organisation. A decision as to where point (c) above can be inserted involves, for example, perceiving that the order in which the writer presents his points is: voting ⎯⎯→ contracts ⎯⎯→ marriage ⎯⎯→ work.

2 Because it deals with passage organisation, it is a coherence exercise. To use it for cohesion practice, give the students the *actual sentences* to be inserted. The students must then think about how what they are adding will fit into the grammatical structure of the passage.

3 Many variations are possible. For example, take a passage and subtract sentences from it. With some sentences missing the passage will be neither coherent nor cohesive. Give it to the students in this form. They must decide where the subtracted sentences fit into the original. Or get the students to do the subtraction: ask them to take points out of a passage and reconstitute it minus these points to form a cohesive and coherent whole.

The point was made earlier that all these techniques aim to *draw attention* to aspects of passage intent and organisation, and that many are something between reading comprehension and writing practice. But many are clearly also just a short step away from what we would more obviously recognise as productive writing practice. The instructions in Example 13 ask the student to *think about* where the points might be made; but by adding the words 'Decide, then rewrite the passage to include these points', the exercise becomes a fully-fledged writing task – and not a particularly easy one at that. Similarly, Example 12 can be given a more productive component by being converted into a 'sentence combining' (SC) exercise. To do this, rewrite the sentences without backward-referring words and present them to the students in this form. Sentence 7 in the example would then become 'In the street the diamond merchant saw a red car by a public telephone'. The student now has two tasks: (a) ordering the sentences, and (b) combining them to form a passage, using appropriate backward-referring words.

SC is a technique much used in America, and is highly productive for practising cohesion.[17] Here is a more straightforward example which does not involve any initial ordering of sentences. The student's task is simply to combine these sentences to form a paragraph:

## Example 14[18]

1　The relationship between managers and workers has changed in Britain.
2　The relationship has changed since the Industrial Revolution.
3　Many of the problems created by the Industrial Revolution are still with us.
4　The Industrial Revolution was nearly 150 years ago.
5　Industrial relations in England are bad today.
6　Why are industrial relations in England bad today?

Three points about this type of exercise:

1　SC exercises are easy to prepare, simply by rewriting passages of any level as strings of sentences without backward-referring words. Sentences containing a lot of information should be divided up into shorter sentences.

2　SC exercises can easily be set up to focus attention on particular cohesive devices which the teacher wishes to concentrate on at a given time.

3　The 'jigsaw principle' (as in Example 12) can always be used, with different students looking at different sentences and coming together to combine them.[19]

SC involves the assembling of passages from individual sentences and is as noted particularly useful for the teaching of cohesion. Assembling and reassembling passages can also be used to teach coherence, an aspect of writing usually associated with the more advanced levels, and one which is only now beginning to be given due consideration.

Here are some assembling and reassembling techniques for teaching coherence:

## Example 15

Parallel writing. Give the students a model passage on one subject, and data (in the form of notes, a diagram, a map, etc.) on a second related subject. The students use this data to write a second page resembling the first as closely as possible.[20] The task can be made as easy or as difficult as required. Johnson (1981) gives data in the form of a second passage. Students must rewrite Passage 2 to have the same structure as passage 1 — a highly complex task.

## Example 16

Reorganising a passage. Choose a passage and think about another way it could have been organised. (For example, the passage in Example 13 could have been organised 'what still needs to be done ⟶ present situation ⟶ past situation' instead of 'past situation ⟶ present situation ⟶

what still needs to be done.' Present the alternative organisation to the students in the form of notes or a plan. Ask them to identify how original and
alternative organisations differ. They then rewrite the passage following the
alternative organisation.

Often it is enough to give the students a revised opening to the passage. Thus we might ask the students to rewrite the Example 13 passage
to begin: 'Women in Britain are without doubt better off today than they
used to be. Today . . . .'

## Example 17

Changing spoken to written English. Because we usually speak in a less
organised way than we write, asking the student to change speech into writing can provide useful coherence practice, as well as drawing attention to
other linguistic differences between the two media. Give the students a trans-
cript of spoken English (from a radio broadcast, listening comprehension
book, etc.) and ask them to turn it into a piece of formal writing.

## Example 18

Changing function or standpoint. The student must rewrite a passage changing its function (from set of instructions to description, for example).[21] The
writer's standpoint can also be changed, though this type of exercise is best
reserved for the advanced level. For example, in the Example 13 passage, the
writer is saying that (although women's position today is better than it used
to be) there is still much to be done. We might ask the students to rewrite the
passage to emphasise that (although there is still much to be done) woman's
position today is better than it used to be.

## 4  Conclusion

A look to the future. There is still much about the teaching of writing
(particularly formal writing of essays, reports, etc.) that is relatively
unexplored. We may make ourselves more aware of the complex processes involved in producing formal prose by monitoring ourselves as
we convert a piece of our own writing (in our L1) from initial draft to
final version. If we note down each change made and attempt to explain
to ourselves why we made it, the full complexity of the operation
becomes apparent. The way we reflect linguistically our decisions to
highlight or de-emphasise points; the way we express concepts to relate
them to, yet distinguish them from other concepts introduced; how we
arrange distribution of old and new information; how we select
synonyms and alternative grammatical structures to avoid inelegant
repetitions – these kinds of (fascinating) processes are little understood
and even less developed through existing teaching materials. Communicative language teaching is generally resulting in a sophistication of
our view of what is involved in language use. But the surface has
indeed only been scratched.

## Notes

1  This is part of an exercise from Morrow and Johnson (1979).

2  This does not of course mean that we should ignore grammar. Bad grammar impedes communication and the student who makes grammar mistakes will often fail to 'get his message across'.

3  As Keith Morrow has pointed out, we can only really say that information is conveyed if the person receiving it does not know it beforehand. There must, in other words, be an information gap. See Johnson (1979) for further discussion of this idea.

4  Or we may simply avoid any 'assigning blame' stage and ask the writer to rewrite his letter even though his initial one may have been perfectly clear and the fault lies with the reader. Writing for an inadequate reader can be a very useful exercise! Asking an advanced student to write something for a low intermediate can impose all kinds of discipline on the writer.

5  Teacher, teacher and students, or students alone will need to look at written work to correct any errors of detail (structural and otherwise). See Brumfit (1977) for suggestions on error correction.

6  The original exercise in Morrow and Johnson (1979) contains a one-part dialogue.

7  From Johnson (1981).

8  To my knowledge, the term 'jigsaw' was first used in language teaching by Marion Geddes and Gill Sturtridge. It is used in Geddes and Sturtridge (1979) for listening; Ronald White also discusses its use for reading (this volume).

9  This topic is touched on briefly by Ronald White at the end of his paper in this volume. For a discussion of this principle in relation to the teaching of speaking, see Johnson (1980).

10  From K and D Johnson, unpublished materials.

11  For discussion of these concepts, and a list of the cohesive devices of English, see Byrne (1979).

12  Some of these techniques are discussed within a more theoretical framework in Johnson (forthcoming).

13  An almost identical procedure is discussed in Raimes (1979)

14  I first heard of this game at the BAAL Seminar on Communicative Methodology (Bath 1977) in a paper by Sidney Whitaker entitled 'ISLEX'.

15  From Michael Newland, *The Diamond Smuggler* in the Ranger Fiction Series (Range 3), (Macmillan Education, 1974). Passages from any reader at any level could be used in this way.

16  Adapted from Johnson (1981), which makes much use of this technique.

17  See Kameen (1978) for further discussion of SC.

18  From Johnson (1981).

19  Byrne (1979: 85) gives an excellent example of 'jigsaw SC'.

20  See Byrne (1979: 45) for an example using a map as stimulus.

21  Widdowson (1973) calls this type of exercise 'rhetorical transformation'.

## DONN BYRNE   Integrating skills

The term 'integrated skills' is frequently used as if it were almost synonymous with reinforcement. Viewed in this way, the process of integrating language skills involves linking them together in such a way that what has been learnt and practised through the exercise of one skill is reinforced and perhaps extended through further language activities which bring one or more of the other skills into use.

Thus, typically, a piece of spoken language, in the form of a dialogue, will be followed by related reading and/or writing activities. Indeed, this pattern – oral work leading onto reading and writing – has become almost the classical model for the organisation of learning materials into 'lessons' or 'units'. The extent to which this is done and the way in which it is implemented, in the form of teaching materials, will be influenced by factors such as the level of the course, the relative importance of the skills for the learners and the view taken of the optimum ordering of the skills but, overall, this kind of skill linking is regarded as pedagogically sound.[1]

However, it may be questioned whether this is the most appropriate model for skill integration in a communicative approach. A unit of work which proceeds, almost inexorably, through listening and speaking activities to reading and writing may provide the teacher with a *convenient* pattern of work to be followed, with some things to be done in the classroom and with others to be done out of class at home (and we expect learning materials to do this to some extent), but it does not get to grips with the problem of how one skill may be actively and meaningfully exercised in order to facilitate and further learning through one or more of the other skills. Nor, as a rule, does it integrate language skills in such a way that the contexts for practising and using all the four skills are established *naturally*. The medium would seem to be the dominating factor: spoken to written language in the early stages and perhaps written to spoken in the later stages (where, however, the pattern is less rigid).

In attempting to outline a communicative approach to skill integration, surely we should keep in mind as a guide the way in which these skills are normally 'integrated' in real life. Here, the use of any skill may lead on quite naturally to the use of another. Reading, for instance, is just as likely to lead to speaking as the reverse. To give a simple example, if we read an ad for a job in the newspaper, we may discuss it with someone (and perhaps leave it at that) or we may ring up and enquire about the job. We may then write a letter of application for the job, which will in turn lead onto somebody else's reading the letter and replying to it. Thus, we have a nexus of READING ⟶ SPEAKING (+LISTENING) ⟶ WRITING ⟶ READING ⟶ WRITING. In short, a whole chain of activities involving the exercise of different language skills has been generated. While none of these is firmly predictable (just as there is no saying where the chain may end), at each point there is a *reason* for language being used in different ways: listening, speaking, reading or writing according to the situation.

In teaching materials the link between one language activity and another has to be contrived to some extent and it is part of the job of the materials writer to do this as effectively as possible. If, therefore, we can build into the materials a mechanism which leads to the exercise of different skills in as natural a way as possible, we shall then be providing the learners with something that is often lacking in the classroom: a *reason* for exercising one skill rather than another. In short, through the contexts provided, the learners will listen, speak, read and write (although by no means necessarily in that order) when it is *appropriate* to do so. In this way it can be expected that not only will their motivation for carrying out the various tasks and activities be improved but also their understanding of the communicative functions relating to each activity increased.

The remainder of this paper will be concerned with illustrating and commenting on this kind of skill integration. In the first example,[2] the 'chain of events' opens with a reading activity. It includes guided as well as free oral expression and involves certain writing tasks. It should be noted that, at the end of the sequence, the learners themselves can decide how it concludes.

1A   *Terry Barnes, a teenager, is getting tired of his job at Holford Natural Products, so he decides to look for a new one. He sees these ads in The Holford News.*

Personnel Manager, HNP, Holford.

**LAB. ASST.** 16-21. **Prev. exp. desirable. Gd. prospects for right person. Trafalgar Tobacco Co. Holford 7997 Ext. 5.**

**JUNIOR ACCOUNTS CLERK to work for Eastern Bus Co. 5 day wk. 9-5.30. Prev. exp. not essential. Typing an advantage. Apply in writing.**

SHORTHAND TYPIST

1B   *Terry first rings up the Trafalgar Tobacco Company. He speaks to the secretary. Listen to their conversation.*

*Secretary*:   Extension 5... Mr Platt's secretary. Who's speaking, please?
*Terry*:   Oh, my name's Barnes. I'm ringing about that vacancy you advertised in The Holford News.
*Secretary*:   Which one was that, now? Was it for a lab assistant?
*Terry*:   Yes, that's right...
*Secretary*:   Well, I'm afraid we've already filled that vacancy. I'm very sorry.
*Terry*:   Have you? Oh, well, thanks very much. Goodbye.
*Secretary*:   Goodbye.

**1C**  *Terry next rings up the Eastern Bus Company. He is told by the secretary that the job is still available, but that he should apply in writing.*
*Make up the conversation between Terry and the secretary.*

**2A**  *Complete this letter which Terry writes to the Eastern Bus Company.* *

---

                                                                July 10

    Dear Sir,

            I am writing to apply for the job of Junior Accounts
    Clerk, which was advertised in The Holford News.

            <u>Now say</u>:  – how old you are

                        – where you are working

                        – what job you do

                        – whether you have had any previous
                          experience of accounts

                        – whether you can type[1]

    My former class teacher at Holford Comprehensive,
    Mr T Newman, will send you a reference if you require one.


                    Yours faithfully,


                    T. Barnes.

---

**2B**  *This is the reply which Terry got from Mr Davis, the manager of the Eastern Bus Company.*

---

                                                                July 16

    Dear Mr Barnes,

            Thank you for your letter of July 10.  I should like
    you to come for an interview on Friday July 23 at 10.30.
    Could you please telephone my secretary and confirm this.

                    Yours sincerely,


                    S. Davis.

---

**2C**  *Terry phones Mr Davis' secretary. He explains why he is ringing and confirms that he can come. Make up the conversation between Terry and the secretary.*

---

* The students have background information about Terry from a previous unit.

3A　*Terry is being interviewed by Mr Davis. Suggest what Terry said.*

*Mr Davis*:　Right, Terry. Sit down. Now, tell me something about yourself.
*Terry*:　　..........
*Mr Davis*:　And how long have you been in your present job?
*Terry*:　　..........
*Mr Davis*:　Really? I'm surprised you want to leave, then.
*Terry*:　　..........
*Mr Davis*:　Well, I've had a word with Tom Newman. But I'd like to speak to your present employers. Is that all right?
*Terry*:　　..........
*Mr Davis*:　Well, thanks very much for coming along. We'll let you know sometime next week.
*Terry*:　　..........

3B　*Mr Davis finally decides to offer Terry the job. This is the letter he wrote.*

```
                                              July 30


    Dear Terry,

         I am pleased to be able to offer you the job of
    Junior Accounts Clerk at a starting salary of £30 a week.
    Would you please confirm that this is acceptable.
    Can you also let us know when you will be free to start?

                         Yours sincerely,


                         Sam Davis.
```

3C　*Write Terry's reply, accepting or declining the job.*

4A　*The following week, Terry meets Carol Davis, a girl he was at school with. Carol is the daughter of Sam Davis. Terry tells Carol what he has been doing recently.*
*Make up the conversation between Terry and Carol.*

4B　*Afterwards, Terry realises that he 'quite likes' Carol. He decides to write to her.*
*Write the letter which Terry sends to Carol.*

4C　*Write Carol's reply.*

Before illustrating further this approach to skill integration, it is perhaps worthwhile commenting on certain features of it. Superficially, it depends on what might be called a 'story-line'. While this is true, what is more important is how the various activities involving different skills are made to flow out of the story-line at various points along the way.

The learners are not made to wait until they have worked their way through a mass of presentation data before being allowed to speak or write for themselves. Secondly, they are given guidance, where this is felt to be appropriate, for both speaking and writing tasks. At a more advanced level, the amount of guidance could be reduced. Thirdly, and this concerns particularly activities relating to the written medium, texts which the learners would find difficult to produce for themselves are given as *reading* material – for example, the letters from Sam Davis – to which they then respond either orally or in writing. Finally, as was pointed out earlier, there is a degree of 'open-endedness' about the sequence which permits the learners to make certain decisions for themselves. In 3C they can accept or decline the job at the Bus Company. Indeed, there is nothing to stop them writing back and asking for a higher starting salary! Similarly, the 'fun' activity at the end of the unit may lead to their writing a passionate love letter in reply to Terry or one giving him the brush-off! Through activities of this kind the learners actually *contribute* to their learning materials.

In the second example below,[3] a conversation provides the setting for a note-taking task, which the learners perform simultaneously with the 'characters'. After this, they are shown, through a *reading* text, how these notes were used to write a notice. They are then asked to write a similar notice for themselves, based on the notes which they have taken. In this way three skills are practised in a fully integrated way through the sequence LISTENING ⟶ LISTENING + NOTE-TAKING ⟶ READING ⟶ WRITING. (Speaking, of course, might also be practised through asking the sudents to act out the conversation.)

**1A** *Bill Halliday (an Australian) and Jane Stokes, his English girlfriend, are planning to go on holiday together. (Bill works in a college bookshop and Jane works in a record shop.) They want to travel round Britain because Bill has not seen much of the country. They are in Jane's flat and they are talking about their plans.*

*Jane*:    ... Well, I don't want to go by train... Why don't we hire a car?

*Bill*:    Hm, it's very expensive, you know. And *you* can't drive! But you've given me an idea! Perhaps we could get a van.

*Jane*:    You mean *buy* one?

*Bill*:    Yes, a secondhand one. One of those big ones...

*Jane*:    But, Bill, they cost a lot... and, besides, there are only two of us.

*Bill*:    Look, we only need about six people. You, me and four more. We can share expenses. It's a marvellous way to see the country – camping, staying in hostels...

*Jane*:    Mm, but how do we *find* six people? Put an ad in the paper?

*Bill*:    No, too expensive. Listen, I'll put a notice up on the board at college. There's one near the bookshop. And what about that newsagent's near the record shop? They have ads in the window.

*Jane*:    OK, then. Well, I suppose we ought to make some notes.....

**1B** *Bill and Jane continue to talk.\* Jane makes notes. Listen – and make a note of the important points.*

*Jane*: Right, here's some paper...and a pen. I'll make the notes.

*Bill*: OK. Well, first...must be able to drive. After all, *you* can't, and I don't want to drive all the time!

*Jane*: ...must be able to drive. And we want people who like a simple life. After all, we're going to camp and stay in hostels.

*Bill*: Yes, definitely no luxuries! Have you got that down?

*Jane*: Hang on! ...no luxuries... Yes, and another thing...they ought to share the cooking too. *I'm* not going to do it all!

*Bill*: ...should be able to cook, then. Right. What else?

*Jane*: Shall we tell them about the cost of the trip?

*Bill*: Mm, yes. Let's say...about £25 each. Plus expenses.

*Jane*: ...£25...and share all expenses. What about age?

*Bill*: Good point! How about...eighteen to twenty-five? And not all English!

*Jane*: Or Australian! So...eighteen to twenty-five...any nationality. *That* should encourage people!

*Bill*: ...Do you think that's all?

*Jane*: Can't think of anything else? We've got quite a lot of notes.

*Bill*: OK, then. *I'll* write out the notice for the board at college...

*Jane*: ...and *I'll* do the one for the newsagent's...

**2A** *This is the notice which Bill put up on the college notice-board the following day.*

# YOU! YOU! YOU! AND YOU!

ARE YOU BETWEEN 18 & 25 ?
CAN YOU DRIVE ? CAN YOU COOK ?

I AM TRYING TO ORGANISE A FOUR WEEK TRIP ROUND BRITAIN IN A VAN — PLACES FOR _FOUR_ MORE PEOPLE

* ANY NATIONALITY WELCOME !
* NO LUXURIES !
* SHARE ALL EXPENSES !
* SMALL CHARGE : £25 EACH

CONTACT : BILL HALLIDAY — COLLEGE BOOKSHOP

\* The students hear the conversation which follows.

**2B** *Now write the notice which Jane Stokes took to the newsagent's. Her telephone number at the record shop is 874 9192 and her number at home is 675 3245.*

It cannot be claimed, of course, that the model presented in the two examples above represents the only possible approach to skill integration in a communicative approach. In practice, if teachers are devising their own materials for integrated skills, they may have to be content with a more simple approach,[4] although it is worth making the point that the underlying mechanism – providing a nexus of activities which bring different skills into play as and when they are appropriate – is not especially complicated to operate and existing teaching materials can be adapted for this purpose. Rather, it is the principle behind this approach that would seem to be especially important: that, in a communicative approach, we should not be trying to get the learners to use the different skills for the purpose of reinforcing one skill through another but rather looking for ways and means whereby we can knit the skills together so that, within the practice contexts provided, they are used in a natural, meaningful and purposeful way.

## Notes

1   This model can be found in a wide range of published courses. It has been considerably modified in some recent courses: for example, Abbs and Freebairn (1977). In this course, reading and writing activities extend rather than reinforce the contexts for learning. Not all the activities, however, develop naturally from previous contexts. For example, in Unit 5, where Jackie writes a note to her mother, the activity is imposed on rather than allowed to develop out of the situation.

2   This example is a modified version of Unit 11 from Byrne and Holden (1976).

3   This example has been taken from Unit 2 of *Going Places* (a post-elementary integrated skills course) by Byrne and Holden (1981).

4   Two recent important articles on integrated skills are by Moulding (1977) and White (1978).

# 2 Procedures and techniques

The four papers in this section focus on practical aspects of what the teacher and students can actually do in the classroom.

Starting with a general consideration and exemplification of the communicative use of visual materials, the section then covers three areas which have attracted particular attention in this field: role-play and simulations, drama, and games and problem-solving. The papers here show clearly how what goes on in a communicatively-orientated classroom is likely to be different from more traditional views of language-learning activity.

Andrew Wright's paper, the first in this section, consists largely of examples of different techniques for employing visuals for communicative practice and production within the areas of speaking and listening comprehension. Many of the techniques he discusses relate closely to the principles elaborated in the Introduction to this part of the book, especially the idea of information-gap. Indeed it might well be argued that the techniques he proposes are communicative precisely (and in some cases only) because they embody this feature. A particularly interesting point arises in the last section of the paper where the writer looks to the future. Talking of the sophisticated technology likely to be available he comments, 'These technical innovations will not play their part if the activity and experience is boring or meaningless to the students . . . . . Nothing is real unless it is felt to be real.'

This question of 'reality' and 'realism' is central to the second paper, *Role-play and Simulation* by Gill Sturtridge. For the author, the chief value of these procedures is their use to reduce the artificiality of the classroom.

Once again the general principles outlined in the Introduction are given concrete form in the examples and discussion. Perhaps the most striking feature of role-play and simulation activities in this respect is the way in which they allow the students *choice* on the level either of what they will say or of how they will say it, or both. Closely connected with this is, of course, the problem of mistakes – what constitutes a mistake and how the teacher should treat it. In many ways this paper illustrates the widening of the horizons of the language teaching classroom which has come to be identified with the communicative movement. Students are no longer confined within the four walls; they are invited to recreate and to simulate events from the outside, real world.

In the same way the next paper, by Susan Holden, represents an extension of the sphere of interest of the language learner and teacher. This time, though, it is an extension beyond language itself into other, closely associated but often neglected, elements of communication. She suggests that through the use of drama techniques, students may be sensitised to the effect of non-linguistic signals which influence the message we communicate just as much as do the words that we use.

This section concludes with a paper by Alan Maley on *Games and Problem-Solving*. Perhaps the main point that the author wishes to get across is that such activities are not just a 'fun', 'wet-afternoon' pastime; rather they are a means of engendering true communication between students. Two crucial characteristics are identified: first the fact that game-like activities allow the learner to be himself without having to adopt an externally imposed role; second, the fact that playing a game is an end in its own right. For the learner playing the game in a foreign language the language ceases to be the 'end' of the activity, and becomes a means to an end. This clearly corresponds to the situation in real language use, where it is not the form of what we say which is the focus of our attention, but rather what we wish to achieve through saying it.

# ANDREW WRIGHT  Visuals

The many established ways of using visual materials – for teaching meaning, for cueing responses in intensive practice work, for indicating some of the meanings of a tense form, for providing cultural background and setting for dialogues etc – are still of use to the teacher with the aims of this book in mind. However, these and many other ways of using visual materials, have been widely described and demonstrated and need not be presented in this short paper.[1] What I do want to do here is to give some examples of areas where the development of materials for a communicative approach has expanded the use of visuals in recent years. These areas are 'Listening Comprehension' and 'Speaking'.

However, before giving examples of the use of visual materials in a communicative approach a number of points should be made:

a)  'visual materials' means anything seen, not just pictures;

b)  the contribution of visual materials to language learning is growing. It has become demonstrably clear that their contribution is relevant to *all* ages, aims and proficiency levels;

c)  although visual materials can be *talked about* quite usefully the most telling role is when they *affect* the student in some way and cause him or her to *want* to listen and to speak. When someone *wants* to listen or to speak there is likely to be a close match between thought and language. The closer this match is the more likely that the language used will be understood and retained.

d) if students are to learn to speak then they must have the maximum opportunity to practise. Working and speaking in small groups or pairs is essential. Visual materials help to direct and promote conversations in groups. It is assumed that in the majority of examples below the activity will move from classwork to group or pairwork.

## 1  Visuals used for listening comprehension

The importance of oral communication in the foreign language is, of course, not only that the participants can express themselves, but that they can understand what the other person is saying.

Visual materials are useful in developing listening comprehension, particularly 'directed listening' (where the student listens for certain information and ignores the rest). They not only help to guide the student's listening, they can provide a general background and context, increase motivation and give evidence of understanding for diagnostic assessment.

## 1.1  Listen and point

The students are asked to identify one picture, from amongst several others, which is related to a spoken commentary or dialogue. (Teacher or tape.)

## Example 1

(A short conversation may be acted out or played on the tape recorder.) The students indicate which people in a crowded picture are most likely to be the ones who are speaking. Of course, several separate pictures may be used instead of one large picture.

## 1.2  Listen and do

Students can be asked to mark, complete, or write on maps, plans, diagrams, pictures, questionnaires, statistical tables, graphs, timetables, pages of diaries and appointment books, etc., according to the information in the text they hear.

## Example 2

The students have a street map either duplicated or projected, and must mark on it a route they hear described on the tape, given by the teacher or fellow student. Of course, a variety of other information might also be given and some of it noted by the student, for example, places of interest to visit.

## Example 3

The students have an information grid for holiday regions and resorts in England. They listen to a text and mark in it the characteristics and amenities for each place they hear.

| | WALKING | HISTORICAL INTEREST | SEASIDE | CINEMA THEATRE | OTHER |
|---|---|---|---|---|---|
| Cambridge | X | ✓ | X | ✓ | Shopping, restaurant |
| Cornwall | X | X | ✓ | X | Warm region |
| Cumberland | ✓ | X | X | X | High rainfall |

## Example 4

The students have a plan of a street which has been the scene of an accident. They mark the plan in different colours according to the statements of various witnesses who describe the position of cars and people at various times.

### 1.3 Listen and draw

The students draw the essentials of what they hear. The drawing might be a plan and route, or a sequence of pictures done with stickmen, or a more detailed drawing.

## Example 5

The teacher reads out a description of a crime, e.g. a bank raid and an eye witness report on the criminals' appearance. Part of the text might be 'He was thin but no taller than the woman. He had long, black hair whereas she had curly fair hair, etc.' The students listen and draw.

## 2 Speaking: controlled practice of conversations

In recent years there have been many ideas developed for the use of magazine pictures for controlled practice. For this reason, only one example is given here, Example 6. [2]

Rather than restate such ideas I feel it would be more useful to give examples of the use of visuals which make people *want* to listen and speak and, to a considerable degree, control what they are thinking of. In this way thought and language are matched. Examples 6 to 9 do provide a considerable degree of control. In Examples 10 to 14 we can predict that certain ideas and language will occur but we cannot be absolutely sure. In these last examples we are moving towards uncontrolled practice and the next section of this paper.

## Example 6

Four to six students have a pile of pictures of holiday regions placed face down on a table. They take it in turns to ask and answer questions according to an example given to them. The answers may be true or false.

*Student A*   B, where are you going for your holidays?
*Student B*   (Picks up a picture, does not show it to the others and decides whether to tell the truth or a lie.) To Egypt.
*Student A*   (Decides B is lying.) I don't believe you.
*Student B*   (Shows his picture of Barbados and gives it to A who has, thereby, 'won' it.)

Student A *might* have said, 'Oh, that's nice'. If B *had* taken a picture of Egypt he would in this case have given it to A.

**Example 7**
Games often cause native speakers to limit their language to certain patterns and functions. Here is one of many examples.

Show about 10 objects, pictures of objects or projected pictures of objects to the students. After two minutes cover the objects and ask the students to say what they remember. Then change the position of one of them and ask, 'What have I done?' The answer will begin, even from most native speakers, 'You've put/moved the.....' etc. Alternatively, remove one of the objects and the answer will be (You've) moved/taken the..... etc.

**Example 8**
In this example the nature of the activity is likely to determine the response and to make the thought and language match very closely. Furthermore, the quality of challenge and the likelihood of different points of view gives a natural, not teacher-determined, reason for communicating.

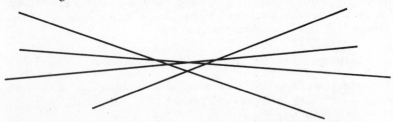

Ask three or four students to draw, in turn, a line on the blackboard or overhead projector. It is better to use a different colour for each line. Then, relying on judgement of the eyes, ask the students 'Which is the longest line?'
    'Is the red line (John's line) longer than the green line (Mary's line)?' etc.
    The lines can be measured to establish who is right. Once more the activity should be done in pairs. Each student criss-crosses a number of coloured lines and asks his neighbour to guess which is the longest, etc.
    Angles and areas may be drawn and judged in the same way.

Although one can confidently predict the need for language to compare lengths one can also predict that other language would be useful if not essential, for example, language to express uncertainty or a point of view, 'I think that . . . .' or 'I *think* that . . . .' or '*I* think that . . . .' etc.

**Example 9**
Devices and methods used for predicting future events are well known. Although it is true that the actual 'seer' often uses a present tense form to stress the immediacy of his or her notion, it is nevertheless normal for lesser mortals to use the future tense form and/or other indicators of future happenings. Horoscopes have now been used in language teaching for some years as they provide a natural context for the use of language forms referring to future events.

Fortunes may be predicted if the teacher brings a current newspaper horoscope (preferably from an English speaking country) to school. The teacher must decide whether to read out the exact wording in the paper or to put the predictions into the language of the syllabus.

'When is your birthday, Jean? – Ah, you'll win some money next week!'

It will be equally natural to use language which refers to past events when discussing whether the predictions have come true.

The use of children's paper fortune tellers or the techniques of palmistry, etc., all help the teacher to move this type of activity to pairwork and to what is, effectively, 'controlled conversation'. If the teacher feels that such ideas are foolish and without foundation then it would be justifiable and indeed intriguing to try them out and use them as a basis for discussion and evaluation!

## Example 10

It can be fascinating to compare two photographs of the same view, taken from the same place, but at two different times. This is particularly the case if one knows the area. One naturally discusses the changes which have taken place and in order to do so the following type of language would prove useful:

This is Church Street today and this is how it used to be.
The butcher's shop used to be a bootmaker's.
The pub was a pub, even then.
It looks as if they've made the walls of this house higher. There are two windows in it now, there didn't used to be.

There will be, almost certainly, a need felt for the language of astonishment,

'It's amazing isn't it?'
'It's hard to believe that....'
'Really?'

Even without photographs, students can be asked to describe the changes they have noted in their area.

## Example 11

Project any slide completely out of focus: a street scene would be very good. Ask the students to suggest what the vague shapes and colours might be. Bring the slide into focus by stages, encouraging speculation and debate at each stage.

This example, like the last, is moving away from *controlled* communicative practice. However, one can predict that language descriptive of place will be required and that this will be put speculatively by some students and more positively by others. Astonishment and request for further elucidation will also be expressed.

**Example 12**

Flash a picture mounted on a card at great speed and challenge the students, 'I'm going to test your reactions (I normally hold the card upside down with its back to the class and then revolve it for a split second only). Once more, the language required is descriptive of place and person (if there are people in it). And, once more, the observations will be put speculatively and doubtfully by some, more positively by others.

**Example 13**

Paste a magazine photograph on the upper half of a piece of card. Cut out several objects or people with the point of a sharp knife. Paste these pieces on the lower half.

Showing only the upper half to the class ask what is missing. The language required will be similar to that in examples 11 and 12.

**Example 14**

Show a slide or a large picture of a street scene for 20 seconds at the same time talking about the doubtful reliability of eye witnesses. Challenge the students to remember all they can about the picture. Remove the picture. The students will require language to describe place, the location of objects and people within the scene, people's appearance and their actions. By the nature of the activity they will refer to what they have seen as a past event. Some students will be speculative and others more positive.

### 3 Conversation, discussion and debate

If we are genuinely interested in the students and in their experiences, opinions and personalities we should, perhaps, avoid describing what they do in terms that smack of pedagogics, however up-to-date. For this reason I have avoided a section title like 'Free Communication Practice'. None of the examples in this section determine the language used. Indeed, the student should be encouraged to make use of all the language at his or her command.

Incidentally, I do believe that genuine conversation can begin in the earliest stages of language learning, however fleeting it might be. When the foreign language is used genuinely, rather than in role play or practice, to request information, to apologise, to describe, to express pleasure, the moment should be cherished, however crude and limited the language might be.

**Example 15**

Collect pictures presenting different aspects of a theme. The ones illustrated on the next page are from a total of six on the theme of travel in this and in the last centuries.[3]

10c

10d

10e

10f

Initially, it is advisable to discuss the content of the pictures to ensure that everyone can recognise what is in them. This activity also gives the students time to interpret what they see, to respond to it, to develop opinions and to remember personal experiences.

Move slowly and naturally into a sharing of these feelings and experiences not imposing a direction to what is said, indeed dropping out of it altogether if possible.

(As a general rule at this stage no one should ever be interrupted if they make a grammatical mistake which does not seriously affect meaning. Make a mental note of the mistake and consider giving explicit practice in it another time.)

**Example 16**

Make a collection of a variety of objects and place them on a table. The objects should be of the type which could be found in someone's pockets and briefcase, for example, bus tickets, museum tickets, meal receipts, scribbled notes of telephone numbers, costs, directions, etc., a small stone (memento?), keys, photo, etc.

*Either:*
Ask the students to work in pairs. They should examine each of the items carefully and then think of a story in which each object occurs. Alan Maley and Alan Duff, in their version of this activity, suggest that, 'as soon as the pair has worked out a story line, they should go over it together making notes and then find another partner. Each student will now retell his story to someone else and, in return, hear a new one. Naturally, they should be encouraged to look for inconsistencies in each other's stories.'[4]

*Or:*
Ask the students, working in pairs or groups of 6, to establish as much about the owner of the objects as possible. After approximately fifteen minutes all the ideas can be put forward and debated until the class as a whole has agreed. Then compare this with your own version. I believe this activity is most effective when the objects *do* all belong to a real person and the students know they are not merely speculating.

**Example 17**

Make a collection of about ten magazine pictures, a few of which should be of rather unusual objects or scenes. Display these on the walls/windows/cupboards, etc. of the room, giving each a number. Ask the students to work in pairs or individually and to think up a story which incorporates each of the pictures in any order. The students can note the order they have chosen by referring to the numbers.

*Alternatively:*
Show four pictures, one by one, to the class as a whole. After seeing the first picture for a few seconds each student should write down the beginning of a story. After five minutes you can ask for some of these to be read out. Show the second picture: the students should continue the story they began with the first but now refer to the second and so on for the four pictures.

Instead of working individually, which stresses the *writing* of the story, students can be asked to work in pairs or groups which will involve language necessary for discussion.

The students will need language to propose ideas and to argue for them, to agree and disagree, to show pleasure, etc., as well as the language of the story itself.

As everyone has made use of the same set of pictures, there will be a reasonable level of interest in the stories when they are read out or told.

## Example 18

Ask the students if they think it is possible to judge someone's age, job, character, etc., by their appearance. Discuss this for a few moments and then show a slide of someone you know, who is unknown to the students. Ask them to suggest details about the person, giving their reasons.

Apart from language necessary to describe the person on the slide there will also be a need for the language of discussion and debate.

This is more than speculative activity. Because judgements can be checked it becomes part of an enquiry into the serious matter of 'getting on with other people'. How much can we judge by physical appearance? What are the dangers of stereotyping and of making easy assumptions? Although there is most certainly a major role for purely speculative activities in language teaching I do believe that the more often the students use the foreign language for matters of importance, the more they will feel that it is an alternative language rather than a foreign language.

## 4  A look at the future

During the coming years video equipment will become increasingly available, giving all the extra qualities of movement, sequence, drama and link between sound and vision. However, these technical innovations will not play their full part if the activity and experience is boring or meaningless to the students. Mere 'realism' offered by television is not enough. Nothing is real unless it is felt to be real.

It might well be that the criss-crossed lines described in Example 8 will present as much meaningful challenge and as authentic a match between thought and language as any more sophisticated presentation.

Used creatively, video can and will make a major contribution: when it is as readily available to the majority of teachers as magazine photographs are now, another paper will have to be written for inclusion in a future edition of this book!

## Notes

1  See for example: Byrne (1976), Moorwood (ed)(1978), Wright (1976).

2  See for example: Rixon (1978), Byrne (1978), Heaton (1971), Kerr (1979), Holden (1978), Wright (1976).

3  From Byrne and Wright (Longman 1975).

4  Maley and Duff (1979).

# GILL STURTRIDGE    Role-play and simulations

Among classroom activities role-play and simulation rate highly as suitable vehicles to use in a communicative approach to language teaching. Used well, they can reduce the artificiality of the classroom, provide a reason for talking and allow the learner to talk meaningfully to other learners.

The terms role-play and simulation have been interpreted in many different ways by teachers and textbook writers, and as simulations involve role-playing, it is best to look first at some different language learning activities that have been described as role-play. The following examples differ from each other in design and in what they allow the learner to achieve in class, but they share to a greater or lesser degree one feature of true role-play: they have an element of freedom of choice for the student. It lies either in a freedom to choose whatever language he pleases or to develop the character or situation as he wishes.

## Example 1

*At the Post Office*

A:  I'd like to post this _____ please.
B:  Put it on the scales. Where to?
A:  To _____ .
B:  That'll be _____ .
A:  _____
B:  _____

This type of exercise is familiar but it *is* role-play in that it differs from the controlled practice of a dialogue or dialogue with slots for the learner to substitute alternatives. It has the element of freedom and a possibility of surprise. B could quote a prohibitive price for sending the parcel or letter and A could decide not to send it. Where there is freedom there is also the opportunity for the learner to experiment — stretching his limited knowledge of the foreign language as he will have to do in real life. It is essential that the learner has this chance at certain points in his language learning programme and that the teacher accepts the probability of error.

This example raises a point about the selection of a role-play situation. Unless B in Example 1 is, or is training to be, a Post Office Clerk he has no experience of the role in his first language and no need of it in the foreign language. On the other hand we must compromise; if we accept that A's role and the situation is relevant to most learners then we must accept B acting as a foil to A. However, the more remote the situation and the roles are from the experience of the learners the more 'unreal' the language they use becomes. For example, a role-play where a policeman confronts a motorist who has parked in the wrong place may provide a lot of fun, but may also result in 'fantasy' language with a very low priority as far as learner's needs are concerned When this happens role-play reaches into the realms of drama and though it provides motivating practice in the foreign language it does not prepare the learner for the situation he might meet outside the classroom. Obviously the situations and roles must be selected with the needs of the students in mind.

A similar danger of overacting may arise when the learner takes the role of a character in the textbook and plays that character in a given situation. He is aware of the personality of the textbook character, his appearance and even the way he speaks. The learner has the support and protection of a mask to hide behind but he will speak as the character in the situation and not as himself. In the following example, on the other hand, the learner is himself and is given guidance as to what to say and how to say it.

## Example 2

*The Invitation*

You meet your friend B at school. You are having a party on Saturday and you would like B to come. The party is informal. Tell B what time to come. Say how glad you are that he is coming.

Cues:

— We're having a party...
   Are you doing anything on Saturday?
— It's very informal...
   Come as you are.
— That's great
   That'll be lovely.

The cues offer an alternative to 'Would you like to come to a party' and if they are new to the learner they change the nature of the activity from using language that he already knows to practising language that he is learning. They also impose language upon him which might not suit his personality: there is a feminine ring to 'That'll be lovely'.

The role-card makes it clear that the learner is a student talking to a friend, a fellow student; the social situation and status of the speakers is clear. This helps the learner to recognise in the foreign language what he instinctively knows in his mother tongue, that different people are addressed in different ways and that he cannot rely on a learnt formula for all situations.

**Example 3**

*Borrowing something*

| A | 2 Friends | B | 2 Friends |
|---|---|---|---|
| Ask B to lend you something | | | |
| | | Ask reason | |
| Give reason | | | |
| | | Agree: add a condition | |
| Agree | | | |
| | | Give object to A (words or action) | |
| Thank B | | | |
| End conversation | | End conversation | |

Here again the relationship is made clear. The learners are given the moves in order and are free to use whatever language they wish. The element of surprise brought in by the information gap between the pair-cards provides something of the spontaneity of a real exchange. It is therefore more in line with a communicative approach than Examples 1 and 2. In classroom management terms though, Example 1 is easier for the teacher in that it can be found in the textbook or written on the blackboard. Examples 2 and 3 on the other hand are designed with an information gap, and wherever information gap techniques are used at least two different role-cards are necessary. The teacher may need to prepare these himself. However, the advantage of pair work cards is that more than one role-play situation can be given out at a time and then pairs of learners can exchange cards when they have finished. In this way the more able learners may complete 3 or 4 exchanges while the slower ones complete only one. The teacher can also grade the difficulty of the situations and give the more difficult pair cards to the more advanced learners. In this way there is some allowance for the individual's level and learning pace.

A disadvantage of the role-card design in Example 3 is that the learn-ers have to be taught the language of the instructions e.g. Agree: add a condition. However, the role-cards do provide the structure of the exchange without imposing any language. This advantage is shared by pictorial role-cards showing events in sequence; these avoid the use of written instructions and are particularly useful with younger learners.

In all these examples the exchange has been very limited; the role-play has provided practice in particular language functions within a nar-row situation. Role-play within a simulation on the other hand allows for extended interaction between learners.

In a simulation the learner is given a task to perform or a problem to solve; the background information and the environment of the problem is simulated. For example the learner is given the information about a town and then told that a new motorway is to be built there. The learner has to discuss the best route for the new motorway. As a learning tech-nique simulations were originally used in business and military training and the outcome of a simulation was of paramount importance. In language learning the end-product, that is the decision the learners reach, is of less importance than the language used to achieve it. The learner, however, must feel that the outcome is important for then he will use language to achieve his objective as he would need to do outside the classroom. This is most obvious in a multi-lingual group where the foreign language is the only means of communication through which the partners or group can work as a team.

In a monolingual group there is the obvious danger that the learners will lapse into their mother-tongue in the excitement. The teacher can bring this problem up with the class and possibly reach an agreement that when one member of a group lapses it is the duty of the others, and in particular the learner to whom he is speaking, to reply in the foreign language. It becomes even more important with a monolingual group to bring as much of the foreign language into the simulation as possible; a foreign language environment must be provided. Alternatively the teacher can recognise the artificiality of a monolingual class working in the foreign language and select simulations where it is *not* the process, that is the decision making, where the language practice takes place but in the end-product. For example the group can be required to use foreign language sources to compile a newspaper or 'radio programme', to do research or prepare a written or oral report. This is not 'surrender', it provides the class with a rehearsal for how they might really work with foreign language sources in their monolingual environment and provides valuable practice in changing from one language to the other.

There are two ways of playing roles within a simulation: with a role-card and without one. When the learner has a role-card it can support him in different ways. It may describe in detail the personality or opinions of the character whose role he is taking. It may tell him how he feels to other members of the group or how to react to a particular situation if it arises. Certain types of interaction, including those less likely to be found in the usual classroom exchanges, can be built into the simulation through the role-card. Hostility or stubbornness which requires strong persuasion can be included.

## Example 4

*The Canbian Educational Aid Project*

S. Dawson A Language Inspector

You are on good terms with your superior, Mr Green, the Chief Language Inspector, although you often disagree with him. However you are ready to argue against anything Mr K. Brown, the Teacher Trainer says as you are old opponents. You want the money to be spent on tapes and tape recorders.
— Point out that the country needs equipment.
— Argue that tape recorders would be easier for inexperienced staff and technicians than language laboratories.

Here Mr Dawson knows his status and relationship with his superior, Mr Green, and that he is not afraid to disagree with him. He also has a clue as to the personality of Mr Dawson who is likely to be somewhat aggressive towards Mr Brown. He is told what his attitude is and given some suggestions as to points he might make during the discussion. While a role-card can provide a mask for the shy learner, it can also have an inhibiting effect upon a learner who receives a role-card which imposes a point of view upon him which he does not share or requires him to act a part alien to him. Role-cards which bring out emotional extremes or acrid disagreement should be avoided. Playing roles can be dangerous and language teachers should step with care in this relatively unknown field.

A simulation which is most likely to give the learner his nearest chance of 'reality' without the stresses of the outside situation is one where no role-card is given and he evolves his own role. In real life we all take 'roles' and are 'different' people depending on whether we are with our family, or friends or the boss. Thus, when no role-card is given the learner faces the task or problem with his partner or the group and his role is determined by his own personality within the group and the job that he does in solving the problem. The learner is most likely to find his usual role when the problem is near to his own experience.

### Example 5

*What are they going to do when they leave school?*

In this simulation a group of secondary school teachers learning English have the task of finding careers for four school leavers. They have details of the careers and openings available and the qualifications, training and characteristics needed for the job. They have to match this information with what they know of the boys and girls from school reports and references. They have to be ready to suggest careers that might suit and interest the school-leavers. The information they receive is both in print and on tape and so they practise both reading and listening skills as they collect the information. No role-cards are given because the teachers are aware of the problems of school-leavers deciding on careers and can give their advice both as people and teachers.

Simulations deserve a more considered place within the teaching programme; they are more than just 'fun' activities or the answer to the conversation class. They are motivating in themselves, they provide a test and feedback on communicative competence and help to develop an empathy between learners; furthermore they provide a 'rehearsal for life'.

## SUSAN HOLDEN   Drama

'Drama' is a convenient umbrella term for activities which involve an element of 'let's pretend . . . .'. These can include role-playing and simulation and also some language games.[1] For the present purposes, however, 'drama' can be said to cover all those activities in which students

a) play *themselves* in an *imaginary* situation

*or*

b) play an *imaginary* person in an *imaginary* situation.

Both these definitions of drama suggest an element of imagination, and this, perhaps, is its value in education generally and in language teaching in particular. It can stimulate the imagination and motivate the student to *use* and *experiment with* the language he has already 'learned'. In order to understand how this can benefit the learner one should, perhaps, consider what happens when two (or more) people are involved in verbal interaction.

Speaking is involved, obviously, and so is listening. But much more than speaking and listening is part of the communicative process. Gestures, facial expression and movement all play their part. Taking an even wider view, it can even be said that one reacts first of all to the way a person looks; provided one understands the outward trappings of a certain culture or society, clothes, haircut and accessories will all be revealing, and will govern the way one addresses the person and reacts to him. In other words, one can well have a visual preconception of a person before he opens his mouth, and tone of voice, gesture and facial expression will reinforce or cause one to adapt this impression. The actual *words* used in the first utterance, whether it comes from oneself or from the other person, will be fitted into this largely visual — and emotional — context. It is rather as if one were moving from long-shot to close-up with a film camera, adjusting one's focus all the time.

'Provided one understands the outward trappings of a certain culture' are the operative words in the paragraph above. One usually associates a large number of mannerisms with certain types of people and behaviour in a culture one is familiar with. Jeans worn in various ways lead one to expect someone to be a student, an 'intellectual', an actor . . . Depending on one's preconceptions of a student or an actor, one will expect any verbal utterance and physical behaviour to follow certain recognisable patterns. Features of intonation and pronunciation, gesture and movement can all be predicted as certainly — or uncertainly — as the *content* of what will be said. But this is only possible if one has learned to 'read the signs' correctly. The oft-quoted example of the Greek nod meaning 'no' is an indication of the confusion that can happen if the signs are not interpreted correctly. Similarly, certain cultures do not expect a bank clerk to wear jeans, or two comparative strangers to kiss each other on both cheeks. If one does not understand these signs one is at a disadvantage, just as if one did not understand the *words* of an exchange, and cannot respond as one would wish.

What does this have to do with language learning, one might ask. The answer would seem to be that, in order to fully understand a speaker from another culture, one should have practice in 'reading the signs' and interpreting the relevant paralinguistic features of any piece of interaction. Most people would agree that such factors as gesture, facial expression and proxemics are a part of verbal interaction: that this should be extended to include clothes and personal appearance may, perhaps, be more startling. However, an understanding of such factors would seem to be a logical extension of that of the more generally accepted list of paralinguistic features which play a part in verbal interaction since one reacts to — or against — them and adjusts one's form of language accordingly.

Apart from these *external* factors, there are other, *internal* ones which are part of each piece of verbal communication. Emotion plays a large part in governing both *what* we say and *how* we say it. 'Emotion' is here taken to mean 'how we feel'. One's feelings are governed by one's mental state — tired, bored, excited; by one's relationship with the other person — hostile, friendly, nervous; one's physical surroundings — public, private, unpleasant, and so on. Emotion makes us hesitate, use a particular register, adopt certain intonation patterns, gesture in a particular way. It is the underlying current that gives form to most pieces of interaction. In other words, language is shaped and coloured by how we feel, and an understanding of this enables us to 'understand' what is being said — and what we are saying ourselves — more clearly.

The significance of this can be appreciated if one thinks of the context in which students often *use* the language they are learning for the first time outside the classroom. One should, perhaps, relate it to one's own first attempts to use a foreign language (or, even, *re-use* it after a period of time). One will be nervous or apprehensive: this makes one worry over much about the form of what one says, and tends to deafen one to what the other speaker is saying. One may not recognise the pronunciation features of the other speaker — and he may not recognise one's own, which is even more upsetting! One may be using the foreign language as a medium of communication with another non-native speaker, so that all one's terms of reference are upset. And, very often, the mundane act of 'asking for information', be it asking for directions, the time a train leaves or how much a hotel room costs will suddenly become real and urgent in a way it rarely is in the classroom. If one only has a limited amount of money, the price of that hotel room or taxi can be crucial, and one's very anxiousness often leads to such tension that one fails to understand or be understood. Communication does not take place or, at least, what is communicated is panic rather than a clear request for information!

The above is a long way of saying that somehow, in our teaching, we should give students practice both in reading the paralinguistic features of the culture group whose language they are learning and in understanding, experiencing and analysing some of the emotions which colour verbal interaction. In this way, we can best help them to transfer from the classroom to the real world. And one of the ways of providing this stepping stone is through drama.

## 1  Ways of using drama

If one accepts the definition of drama in the first paragraph of this paper, and one agrees with the dual aims of *accustoming the student to reading the paralinguistic signs of behaviour* and *experiencing and analysing emotions* as an aid to better communicative interaction, then one has to devise some exercises which will provide practice in these.

Perhaps the simplest way is first to focus on pieces of interaction where movement, facial expression and gesture are the factors which carry the communication: no words are used.

### Example 1

*To illustrate how much can be conveyed without words*
Ask the students to work in pairs or small groups (maximum 5 students per group). Each student takes it in turns to pick up an imaginary object from the floor without saying anything. The other students can try to guess what the object is, and may ask any necessary questions: 'Is it heavy?' 'Do you like it?' 'Have you got one?', etc. It should, however, be fairly easy to guess at least the *type* of object from the way it is picked up and held, while the facial expression will reveal something of the student's attitude towards it.

The important thing is for the students to realise they must be absolutely clear about the object before they 'pick it up'. In other words, they must decide what it looks like, what it feels like, where it is – and also define their own attitude towards it. Maybe it is rather disgusting – a piece of old chewing gum; or something they would like to keep – a banknote. Of course, if it is a banknote, there may be conflicting emotions as they pick it up. 'Shall I keep it? If I do, I can . . . But it's not mine. Someone else may be looking for it . . .' All this may be conveyed to the watchers through facial expression and gesture. But this will only happen if the students are encouraged to be absolutely clear and specific about both the object and the emotion.

Generally, with this exercise, students are interested to see how much they can convey without using words. They may also be interested to try the exercises again, trying to convey different emotions about the same object. The discussion which follows the miming is an integral part of the activity: it gives language practice as well as helping the whole group focus on the outward signs of the emotion. If the group become very interested in the activity, this interest may lead them to use their own language (in a monolingual group) rather than the target language. It is for the teacher to decide how important this is; obviously it is something which must be controlled, but it can be beneficial if the students gain a deeper understanding of these aspects of communication through extended discussion.

## Example 2

*To illustrate the effect of feeling on an interaction activity*
The students work in pairs. They are both watching a television programme. One student turns it off. The other reacts. The first time the exercise is done, this reaction should be non-verbal; once the underlying emotion and the means of communication have been established, appropriate words should be added.

The interest of this exercise lies in the way in which the students are able to convey their feelings clearly to each other. It should be impressed upon them that each pair should establish *what* they are watching and *where* they are before they begin, since these two factors will affect their behaviour. Then the appropriate person in each pair should decide for himself *why* he turns off the programme or *what* his attitude to the programme is (which will obviously affect the way he reacts). At this point, both students are playing themselves, but they are interacting in an imaginary situation outside the classroom: the nature of the surroundings – hotel lounge, crowded bar or their own flat – will influence the words and gestures used as well as the extent to which they obviously 'show' their feelings.

It will be noted that no mention has been made of the 'performance' factor in dramatic activities. Both the activities outlined above entail all the students in the class taking part at the same time. And, what is more, taking part as themselves. As Gill Sturtridge says in her paper, it is very easy to set up situations in which the students act or role-play ticket clerks and policemen. But such a role-play can never be more than an impersonation. It serves little real purpose unless the students have experience in real life of these roles, or are going to need it. And, since they are unlikely to know much about the reality of such roles in a foreign culture, any such impersonation is likely to be very superficial and lacking in real motivation. It would seem much more valuable for students to begin from the starting point of their *own* emotions and the ways of expressing them, and not to try to add the complicating factor of interpreting another person until they have had extensive practice.

As far as 'performance' is concerned, different teachers and students react in different ways to it. One danger is that the mere fact of performing in front of the class often inhibits some students, while it makes others 'show off' and become very superficial. It is probably best for each teacher to decide what will most benefit a particular class at a particular time. Certainly students often ask to 'show' their scenes, and this request should not be refused — although it is wise to remember that the rest of the class may not be particularly interested! A compromise situation is for the various pairs and small groups to combine into larger groups of 8–10 students so that any 'presentation' is done within the larger group rather than to the whole class.

## 2 Extended dramatic activities

It will be noticed that the two examples above are both very short: sometimes they take only 10 minutes to do, although if much discussion results, then the activity may well extend to 20 or 25 minutes. Given the crowded nature of most syllabuses, short meaningful activities which can be adapted to various language levels (necessary in classes of mixed ability) are more useful than longer ones. At times, however, student interest may be such that it seems worthwhile setting up an extended 'improvisation' which will allow greater scope for invention and experiment.

It is wise, however, to start in the same small way with a pair of students establishing their basic motivation and trying out the most effective form of communication. In this way, each piece of interaction will be more carefully thought out. And each stage of the improvisation can still occupy about 10 or 15 minutes of successive lessons, and the whole activity can be brought to a halt quite naturally if it seems to have lost any learning value.

### Example 3

*To give students the opportunity to build up more complex relationships*
The class is divided into groups of about 10 students, and these constitute the 'working groups' for the activity. In a small class, there may well be only one group. All the students are guests — or hosts — at a party. They can play either themselves or another character. If they choose to be another character, they should spend some time deciding exactly who they are, and then 'present' themselves to the rest of the group. This may involve the use of visuals, and can become an interesting project in its own right, as the rest of the group ask them questions about themselves and their lives. The group should decide which people are giving the party.

The second stage is to try and work out relationships between various pairs of party guests. The students can practice activities such as introducing themselves to someone they do not know, asking a friend to do them some kind of favour, or inviting a stranger to go out with them. Each piece of interaction should be kept short, and the students should aim for *total* communication; gesture, movement and facial expression will help them establish and reinforce their own characters and help them to interpret those of other people.

The party is built up through various stages, combining several pairs of students together in varying permutations and giving them a specific piece of interaction to work on. If it seems appropriate, an 'event' can be introduced: two people can have an argument, someone can feel ill... Some teachers and students may prefer the more obviously 'dramatic' type of event — a police raid or a serious accident. The only thing to remember is that with this, as with all dramatic activities, it is usually best to 'start small' and establish character and relationship before too many external factors are introduced.

Activities such as those outlined above may seem a time-consuming luxury in an overcrowded syllabus. However, the possibility of gaining some *real* insight into the communicative process would seem to make them more worthwhile than a superficial 'acting out the dialogue' in the front of the rest of the class.

A final comment is that dramatic activities of this kind are fun for most people, and they do not demand any great acting ability. This is something to remember when assessing various activities: care should be taken not to choose ones which ask the students to do things they could not — or would not want to — do in their own language. However, if that danger is avoided, most students will relax and concentrate on achieving meaningful communication in the given context, thus gaining practice which will prepare them for the unknown features of communication outside the classroom.

## Note

1   See the papers by Gill Sturtridge and Alan Maley in this book.

# ALAN MALEY   Games and problem solving

## 1  Introduction

Games and game-like activities have an obvious and important place in
a theory of language learning based on the development of 'communicative competence'. If we accept that all classrooms are unlike the outside
'real' world in important respects, we cannot expect to replicate 'real
situations' in the classroom except through some kind of conjuring trick
involving the temporary suspension of disbelief. The kinds of activities
described below do foster 'natural', 'creative', 'authentic' language
behaviour on the part of learners once the framework of rules and conventions has been firmly established. The games themselves are not
real' in the sense of being replicas of the kinds of activities learners will
be involved in outside the classroom. What goes on within the fictitious
framework the game provides *is* however genuine language behaviour
and involves the use of functional categories which will have much
wider application.

Such activities differ from role-play in the kind of language behaviour
produced. In game-like activities the learner is free to be himself. He
can engage his real personality with those of his fellow-learners without
the additional burden of trying to be someone else. The kinds of things
he says have not been pre-programmed (though, as we shall see below,
they are partially predictable).

In role-play and more formal techniques, student output tends to be
equated with teacher input. Here however, the student output depends
upon real interaction with other learners within a prescribed set of conventions. Any input, in the form of rules, instructions, information has
to be processed by the learner before he can act upon it. More importantly perhaps, the learner's attention is diverted from the language to
the task/activity in hand. Language becomes a necessary tool, but is no
longer the unique end.

It would be contended that such activities facilitate the *acquisition* of
the foreign language rather than its *learning*. These two terms are being
used in a rather special sense, *acquisition*[1] being characterised as largely
unconscious, peripheral,[2] effortless, 'whole-person'[3] and deeply rooted,
*learning* as consciously involving effort, at the centre of the learner's
field of concentration, external to his personality, shallow and relatively
easily forgotten. (Space does not allow for a detailed discussion of this
problem but it is central to the whole business of how it is that foreign
languages come to be learned.)

Whether or not one agrees with this contention, what is certain is that
the activities described below are firmly in the realm of language *use*
rather than language *learning*. They need therefore to take place in an
atmosphere which is non-judgmental and where the teacher occupies a
peripheral position.

## 2 Typology

Sharp distinctions are difficult to make between games and problem-solving activities. At its best a game involves some element of conscious choice and problem-solving, in however small a way. Nor will any really useful problem-solving activity fail to entertain in a game-like way. Both types of activity have 'outcomes' of some kind: in games this is more likely to be a winner or a result, in problem-solving, a solution. Games more often appeal to the affective part of our consciousness, problem-solving to the cognitive part. But both aim to create and utilize an 'information gap'.[4]

The tentative groupings set out below are accordingly simply for the sake of convenience and should not be taken as having any deeper significance than that.

### 2.1   Games

a)   based on observation, (and memory) e.g. You are a witness.
b)   based on interpretation (and guessing) e.g. Blurred focus, Back writing.
c)   based on individual/group interaction e.g. The Name Circle.
d)   board games e.g. Monopoly, Diplomacy etc.
e)   card games e.g. Tarot.
f)   pencil and paper games e.g. Consequences etc.

### 2.2   Problem-solving activities

a)   based on information transfer e.g. 'Mais t'es ma femme!', split dialogues/stories, Tangram.
b)   based on decision-making e.g. Front Page, Ambiguous dialogues/sound sequences.
c)   based on logic e.g. Paradoxes, High Noon etc.

Each of these types of activity will now be described.

## 3   Activities

### 3.1   You are witness

Students are told they will be witnessing an event which they will subsequently have to remember and report on in detail. A colour slide is then projected for a very brief lapse of time (e.g. 5 seconds). Each student individually writes down what he remembers. Small groups are then formed to compare notes. Finally the slide is shown again for comment, comparison with reports, and discussion.

An alternative procedure is to form groups at the outset and to give each group a picture to look at together briefly. The picture is then taken away and the group remembers it together. Thereafter each group receives another group's picture and 'interrogates' a member of the group from which it came.

### 3.2 Blurred focus

A very poorly focussed colour slide is projected. It should be possible barely to make out blobs of colour. In pairs, students speculate about what they can see. The focus is then sharpened slightly. Students speculate again, changing their previous opinion if appropriate. The procedure continues until the slide is sharply focussed.

### 3.3 Back writing

In pairs students trace a short message with their fingers on their partner's back. The message can be left to the students to invent. Alternatively if the teacher wishes to tie the communication game in with structural or lexical items presented more formally, he can distribute cards to each student with messages already written on them.

The game can be done with numbers or pictures as well as with sentences.

A variation is to form a circle with each person facing his neighbour's back. The teacher gives a written message to two or three of the students. They then begin to write it on the back of the person in front of them. The messages are passed round the circle until they come back (often unrecognisable!) to their point of origin.

### 3.4 The Name Circle

Students sit in circles of about 10 people. One person starts off by giving his first name and an invented profession (e.g. I'm Fred and I'm a welder). The next person has to repeat this information (i.e. You're Fred and You're a welder) and add in himself (I'm Jane and I'm a reporter). The game proceeds cumulatively until it comes back to 'Fred' who has to repeat the whole sequence.

Clearly this is open to almost unlimited variation, since the 'profession' can be replaced by almost any other kind of information, real or imaginary (e.g. I like, I hate, I come from...etc.)

### 3.5 Board games

Space does not allow detailed description of those which are commercially available. Before adopting one for the foreign language classroom however it should be tried out for level of difficulty, and usefulness as a communication activity involving language. (Many such games are complex and can be played almost silently.)

An example of a specially devised ELT board game is 'Take a chance with questions!'.[5] This is played in pairs on this board.

| Start Finish | Where | How | Who | Chance | What | ? |
|---|---|---|---|---|---|---|
| Why | | | | | | How |
| How | | | | | | Go on 2 squares |
| When | Who | Word | Number | How | | When |
| Chance | | | | | | Where |
| ? | When | **TAKE A CHANCE WITH QUESTIONS** | | What | | Why |
| Who | | | | | | What |
| Sorry, miss a chance | Why | Picture | Chance | Where | | Another chance |
| Who | | | | | | ? |
| Where | | | | | | Who |
| What | | | | | | How |
| How | Why | Take a chance | What | When | Go on 3 squares | Where |

Before starting, players pick a card from the picture, word or number pile. They throw dice alternately and move their counters accordingly. If they land on a 'what' square for example, they take a card from the 'what' pile in the centre. This contains a question which must be combined with the information on their picture, word or number card which they must answer. If the answer is satisfactory to their partner (or the group) they keep the card. The winner is the person with most cards at the end, not the one who finishes first. Chance cards feature any specific items the teacher wishes to introduce.

## 3.6   Tarot

The traditional Tarot packs are too complex for story-building games.[6] Their potential for re-combining the essential elements of all stories (cf. the Propp list) has however been realised in a set of Tarot cards, specially created for language learning. The cards are coded for various of the story elements (e.g.

hero, wishes, obstacles, enemies, etc.) and the pictures on them are sufficiently ambiguous for individual students to give different detailed interpretations.[7]

## 3.7 Consequences

In its 'pure' form this consists of each player writing first the name of a male protagonist at the top of a sheet of paper. This is then folded and passed on to the next person. Each player then writes 'met X' (a female person's name) folds the paper again and passes it. The game proceeds in this way with these stages:

where they met
what she said to him
what he replied
what the result was

When the papers are unfolded and read out there is usually general hilarity!

The principle of the game is open to great variation. For example, in pairs, each writes a 'why' question, folds the paper and passes it to his partner. Then each writes a 'because' answer.

In groups of five, each writes the answer to the questions Who? What? How? When? Where?, folding and passing each time.

The absurd and unusual results of this kind of game can lead into profitable discussion, story-building, role-play and further writing.[8]

## 3.8 Mais t'es ma femme!

Each student is supplied with a card on which some personal information is recorded in brief form in two columns.
e.g.

| Me | Her |
|---|---|
| Jack | Madge |
| 30 | 25 |
| lorry driver | Secretary |
| London | London |
| Supports | Costa Brava |
| West Ham | Holiday 1978 |

| Me | Him |
|---|---|
| Madge | Vic |
| 25 | 65 |
| Secretary | retired |
| London | heart trouble |
| Costa Brava | |
| Holiday 1978 | London |

Students are told to find the person described on the left of the card. This involves asking questions of the other people in the game. It is not possible to assume the right person has been found until *all* the information is exhausted, since the cards are prepared in such a way that there are two Jacks, two Madges etc. and they differ from each other in only *one* fact. The activity is further complicated by the fact that though Jack is looking for Madge, Madge is not looking for him! The game ends when everyone has been found and discovers that he belongs to a family (or other group). This too is open to variation since almost any kind of information can be recorded on the cards: colours, numbers, fruit, place names, scientific and technical apparatus etc.

### 3.9 Split dialogues

A series of two-line dialogues is cut *up into individual utterances*
e.g.

1  A  What are you doing?
   B  What's that got to do with you?
2  A  How's he feeling?
   B  No idea.

These are distributed at random, one to each participant. The activity consists in finding the other half of your dialogue. Normally more than one solution is possible and in the round-up session interesting new combinations are revealed.

A variation on this is to cut up a written text (story, newspaper article etc.).

Each group is given a piece. Groups make a summary of what their extract says. Then the group which thinks it has the beginning reads out its summary. The group which thinks it leads on then reads, and so on.[9] When everyone is satisfied that the pieces are in the right order, the complete text is distributed.

### 3.10  Tangram

The Tang is a Chinese game consisting of seven pieces.

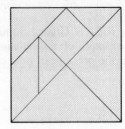

These can be formed into an infinity of shapes, both figurative and non-figurative.[10]

A number of problem-solving activities can be based on this versatility. Here are three:

a) In groups of three, students are given an outline shape and have to discover together how the pieces fit into it.
e.g.

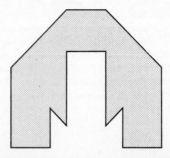

This done, they write instructions on how to form this shape for another group. Groups then exchange instructions and try to make the shape.

b) In pairs, A has the pieces, B a diagram.
e.g.

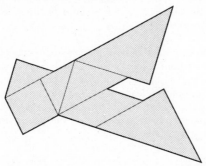

B gives oral instructions to A. (Needless to say A cannot see B's diagram.)

c) A shape is assembled in a corner of the room. Each group appoints a reporter, who is allowed to go and look at the shape as often as he likes but cannot touch it or make a diagram. His job is to give instructions to his group leading to a successful assembly of the shape.[11]

## 3.11 Front Page

'Front Page' is one of the ILEA 9 Graded Simulations, now unhappily out of print. It is a good example of a simulation in which group decision making goes on under the pressure of time constraints.

Groups represent editorial teams on a local newspaper. After reading sheets concerning editorial policy etc. they are issued with a succession of articles and have to decide which they will place on a blank but blocked-out front page format. There would be no better example of an activity where concern about the language recedes into the background and the task takes over. There are further references to simulations of this sort in the bibliography.

## 3.12 Ambiguous dialogues

In groups students listen to dialogues of the following type:[12]

1 A If you like, but I think it's unwise to let him out so soon.
  B But he must get out sooner or later.
  A I'm not sure he's ready, yet.
  B Nor am I, to be quite honest, but the longer he stays here the harder it gets.
  A You're right, I know. All the same, it worries me.

2 A He must get out.
  B Not yet. Please, Fred. Not yet.
  A He can't go on staying here.
  B Fred, I'm so frightened...
  A I'll be with him.
  B But you never know what might happen.

3   A   I'm taking him away.
    B   Well, I can't stop you.
    A   You don't approve, do you?
    B   I can't say that I'm happy about it.
    A   But look how long he's been here. And what difference has it made?
    B   It takes a long time, you know...But do as you wish.

They are invited to speculate about the contextual features of the interaction: who is speaking to whom, what their relationship (role/status) is, where they are, who or what they are talking about, what will happen next etc.

Discussion of these factors leads into role-play of parallel situations.

A variant of this activity is to replace the dialogue with a sequence of sound effects.[13] In this case students speculate on the nature and sequence of the events they imagine they have heard.

### 3.13   Paradoxes

The essence of the paradox is that it states something which must be false if it is true, and must be true if it is false. It is therefore favourable terrain for almost endless discussion.

One example must suffice:

'Once upon a time a lawyer called John borrowed £1000 from another lawyer called James. He promised James that he would pay it back as soon as he won his first case in court. But as John was very lazy he never took a case at all. After a year or two James got fed up and decided to take John to court to force him to repay his debt. When the day of the trial came both John and James felt very confident. John was sure that, whatever happened, he would not have to pay. James was sure he would recover his money. Which of them was right?'

Groups are asked to make up their mind on this one and then to compare results!

### 3.14   High Noon – a logical problem

Again, only one example of this kind of problem can be given.[14] It is designed to be done as a group task, with a written explanation of the solution if this is felt desirable.

The main street in Coffin Canyon was dusty and the sun shone down pitilessly as the seven bandits came out of the saloon. They had been drinking all morning and had got into an argument about who was the best shot. The only way to solve this problem was to go into the street and shoot it out. So they all staggered out into the blinding sun and took up position as in the diagram below. Their names were Al, Butch, Chuck, Dude, Eric, Fred and Gus. You can see where they were standing from the diagram on the next page. As you can see, each man could take a shot at just two others. So without moving from their positions they began firing. Dude fell down dead first, shot through the head by Al. In fact Al was the only one left alive at the end of the battle. From this information you can work out who shot whom and in what order the six men were killed.

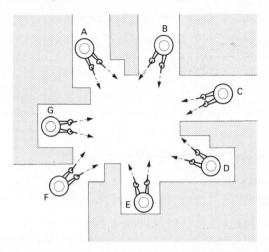

## 4 Choosing an activity

a) One criterion which needs consideration is the proportion of input to output involved in a given activity. By input I mean text, visuals, instructions, apparatus etc. By output, what students will need to do with the input and the extent to which this will involve them in oral or written interactions which are their own. If we look at the activities described above (section 3) they can be divided into the following profiles:

**i) high input + high output**
e.g. Front Page. Students have a great deal of reading to do before they can engage (and while they are engaging) in their oral/written interactions.

**ii) low input + high output**
e.g. Blurred focus or ambiguous dialogues. Here a minimal stimulus sets off a high degree of oral interaction.

No examples have been given of the other possibilities:

**iii) low input + low output**
e.g. noughts and crosses, which can be done almost silently.

**iv) high input + low output**
e.g. logical problems which involve a long reading text but which can be done individually without interaction.

Clearly, in a communicative teaching programme, activities will be chosen which conform to profiles i) and ii). One advantage of high input is that it often provides students with some of his verbal ammunition for the output stage. Profile iv) has its place in a programme where, for example, reading and deductive skills are of high importance.

b)   Other criteria which need to be taken account of would be:

i)   the need to create an information gap which can only be filled by genuine interaction.
ii)   the need to involve students in doing as well as saying.
iii)   the need for the activity to be satisfying or interesting.
iv)   the need for a pay-off in terms of the language the activity will require for its satisfactory completion.

## 5  Activities and the language they generate

All the activities described in Section 3 and others of their kind give rise to certain types of language, which can be predicted to a greater or lesser degree.

In certain of the games e.g. The Name Circle, Consequences, there is a high degree of control over this – the game in fact consists in uttering sentences of a given form in a given order.

In others it is not possible to control the language output to this extent. It is however possible to predict that certain kinds of language act will be involved, for the activity depends upon them for its successful termination. Let us take as an example the group interaction which takes place in solving the logical problem 'High Noon'!

i)   language needed for group organisation

| | | |
|---|---|---|
| Proposing/suggesting | e.g. | Let's X |
| | | Why don't we Y? etc. |
| Agreeing/disagreeing | e.g. | Yes. O.K./No. Not yet. |
| Asking for information | e.g. | Have you got a pen? |
| Asking for clarification | e.g. | What should we do first? |
| Asking for confirmation | e.g. | So, you'll keep a record, O.K.? |

ii)   language needed for solving this particular problem:
e.g. Logical consequences

If A shot D then E must have been . . . . . . .
He can't have shot 3, otherwise he would have . . . . etc.

iii)   language for taking, keeping and ceding the right to speak.

| | | |
|---|---|---|
| e.g. | Directing | Right |
| | | What do you think? |
| | | How about you? |
| | Interrupting | Just a minute. |
| | | Hold on. |
| | | Hey, Wait a minute. |
| | | Can I just . . . . .? |
| etc. | | |

This is by no means exhaustive but it does give an idea of the kind of linguistic patterns needed for the successful performance of this particular activity. Whether these are presented to students before, or after the activity takes place is a matter of choice.

## 6 Conclusion

The games and activities presented here offer a role-structure within which creativity, in it widest sense, can operate. However 'unreal' or 'artificial' they may be in themselves, the interactions to which they give rise are genuine ones.

## Bibliography

Books and articles to which reference is made in the text of this paper are referenced in the main bibliography for this book. Here, though, is a short bibliography of works relevant to this topic which are not specifically mentioned in the text.

ANDERSON, V and BEREITER, C  *Thinking Games 1, 2, 3* (Ontario Institute for Studies in Education)

BRITISH COUNCIL, *ELTI Materials Profile 4: Communications Games*

BRITISH COUNCIL, *Games, Simulations and Role-Playing* (ELT Documents)

DE BONO, E  *The Five-Day Course in Thinking* (Penguin)

FIX, J F  *Games for the Super-Intelligent* (Muller)

HEID, M and MALEY, A (eds)  *Kreativitat in Fremdsprachen Unterricht* (Goethe Institut Munchen Werkheft 1976) Collected conference papers – many in English

HEID, M and MALEY, A (eds)  *Rollenspiel und Simulation* (Goethe Institut Munchen Werkheft 1977)

HEYWORTH, F  *The Language of Discussion* (Hodder and Stoughton)

HUGHES, P and BRECHT, G  *Vicious Circles and Infinity – An Anthology of Paradoxes* (Penguin)

KERR, J Y K  *Picture Cue Cards* (Evans)

MALEY, A, DUFF, A and GRELLET, F  *The Mind's Eye* (CUP) ·

MANAGEMENT GAMES LTD, 11 Woburn Street, Ampthill, Bedford for lists of business simulation games

PFEIFFER, J W and JONES, J E  *A Handbook of Structured Experience for Human Relations Training Vols 1-IV* (University Associates Publishers and Consultants, La Jolla, California)

POTE, M et al  *A Case for English* (CUP)

RINVOLUCRI, M et al. *Challenge to Think* (Pilgrim's Language Courses, Publishers)

RODARI, G  *Una Grammatica della Fantasia* (Einandi, Torino)
SAGSET,  Centre for Extension Studies, University of Loughborough
  for list of Resource Lists on Games and Simulations
TRIM, J and M  *Sounds Right* (CUP)
WAKEMAN, A  *Jabberwocky* (Longman)
WRIGHT, A et al  *Kaleidoscope* (Macmillan)
WRIGHT, A et al  *Games for Language Learning* (CUP)

## Notes

1  See Krashen (1977).

2  See Lozanov (1978).

3  See Stevick (1976) and Curran (1972).

4  See Keith Morrow's paper earlier in this part of the book.

5  This was developed by Rosalind Page at the British Council in Paris (unpublished).

6  Though see Italo Calvino *Il Castello dei Destini Incorociati* which is based entirely on combinations of the Tarot.

7  See *Le Tarot des Mille et Une Cartes* by Francis Debyser. (L'Ecole des Loisirs, 8 rue de Sèvres, Paris 7ème).

8  See Caré and Debyser (1978) and Maley (forthcoming).

9  An activity developed by S F Whittaker of the University of Bangor.

10  See Elffers (1977).

11  I owe the original version of this activity, involving Lego, to Jack Lonergan of the Pedagogische Arbeitstelle of the Deutsche Volkshochschulverband.

12  This is taken from *Variations on a Theme* by A Maley and A Duff by kind permission of CUP.

13  See Maley and Duff (1977) and (1979).

14  Reprinted from *Mind Matters* by A Maley and F Grellet (forthcoming) by kind permission of CUP.

# References

ABBS, B and FREEBAIRN, I *Starting Strategies* (Longman 1977)

AHRENS, P (ed) *Tense Time*, Vols. 1, 2, 3, (Longman 1977)

ALATIS, J E and TWADDELL, K (eds) *English as a Second Language in Bilingual Education* (TESOL, Washington D.C. 1976)

ALEXANDER, L G *Mainline Skills A* and *B* (Longman 1973)

ALEXANDER, L G and KINGSBURY, R H *Follow Me 1* (Longman 1980)

ALLEN, J P B and WIDDOWSON, H G 'Teaching the communicative use of English' (*International Review of Applied Linguistics*, 12/1, 1974) and in BRUMFIT and JOHNSON (eds) (1979)

ALLWRIGHT, R L 'Language Learning through Communication Practice' (*E L T Documents* 76/3, 1976) British Council and in BRUMFIT and JOHNSON (eds) (1979)

ARNOLD, J W and HARMER, J *Advanced Speaking Skills* (Longman 1979)

BROUGHTON, G 'A study of the teaching in pre-Secondary state schools of EFL in France and Germany, with particular reference to teaching materials in current use, and the linguistic and pedagogic assumptions on which they are based' (PhD thesis, University of London 1972)

BRUMFIT, C J 'Correcting Written Work', (*Modern English Teacher, 5/3* 1977)

BRUMFIT, C J 'Review of D A Wilkins Notional Syllabuses' (*BAAL Newsletter* 5, 1978) Reprinted as 'Notional Syllabuses: a reassessment' in *Problems and Principles in English Teaching* (Pergamon 1980)

BRUMFIT, C J and JOHNSON, K (eds) *The Communicative Approach to Language Teaching* (Oxford University Press 1979)

BURSTALL, C JAMIESON, M COHEN, S HARGREAVES, M *Primary French in the Balance* (National Foundation for Education Research, Slough)

BYRNE, D *Teaching Oral English* (Longman 1976)

BYRNE, D *Materials for Language Teaching 1, 2 and 3* (MEP 1978)

BYRNE, D *Teaching Writing Skills* (Longman 1979)

BYRNE, D and HOLDEN, S *Insight* (*Longman 1976*)

BYRNE, D and HOLDEN, S *Going Places* (Longman 1981)

BYRNE, D and WRIGHT, A *What Do You Think?* (Longman 1975)

CARE, J M and DEBYSER, F *Jeu, Language et Créativité* (Hachette/Larrousse 1978)

COULTHARD, M *An Introduction to Discourse Analysis* (Longman 1977)

COUNCIL of EUROPE *Systems Development in Adult Language Learning* (1973)

CURRAN, C A *Counselling-Learning: a whole person model for education* (Grune and Stratton, N.Y. 1972)

DAVIES, A 'Textbook situations and idealised language'. Paper delivered at the AILA/BAAL Seminar on The Communicative Teaching of English, Lancaster 1973 (Mimeo)

DERRICK, J et al. *SCOPE Stage 1: an introductory English Course for immigrant children* (Longman/Books for Schools 1969)

DONLEY, M 'The Paragraph in Advanced Composition: a Heuristic Approach' (*English Language Teaching Journal*, 30, 1976)

VAN EK, J A  *The 'Threshold Level' in a Unit/Credit System* (Council of Europe 1973)

VAN EK, J A  *The Threshold Level* (Council of Europe 1975)

VAN EK, J A  *The Threshold Level for Schools* (Longman 1978)

VAN EK, J A and ALEXANDER, L G *Waystage* (Council of Europe 1977)

ELFFERS, J  *Tangram: The Ancient Chinese Shapes Game* (Penguin 1977)

GARVIE, E *Breakthrough to fluency* (Blackwell, Oxford 1976)

GEDDES, M and STURTRIDGE, G *Listening Links* (Heinemann 1979)

GEDDES, M. and WHITE, R V 'The use of Semi-scripted Simulated Authentic Speech and Listening Comprehension' (*Audio-Visual Language Journal* 16/3, 1978)

GUMPERZ, J J and HYMES, D (eds) *Directions in Sociolinguistics* (Holt, Rinehart and Winston 1970)

GUTALE, E 'Early reading activities and their bearing upon the backing of EFL at Primary level'. Paper delivered at the 1975 IATEFL Conference. (Reported in *IATEFL Newsletter* 41, January 1976)

HALLIDAY, M A K *Explorations in the Functions of Language* (Edward Arnold 1973)

HAWES, H *Curriculum and Reality in African Primary Schools* (Longman 1979)

HAWKES, C N 'Some considerations of principle for TEFL in the European Primary School' (*ELT Documents* 74/3, 1974 The British Council)

HAWKES, C N 'The medium of instruction in Primary Schools in Ghana' (*West African Journal of Modern Languages*, Ibadan 1976)

HAWKES, C N and BEZANSON, K A 'Bilingual reading skills of Primary School children in Ghana (*Working Papers on Bilingualism*, 11, Toronto, 1976)

HAWKES, C N, MACAULEY, J I and DALLAS, D A *Nigeria Primary Eng-. lish* (Longman, Nigeria 1979)

HEATON, B *Practice Through Pictures* (Longman 1971)

HOLDEN, S (ed) *Visual Aids for Classroom Interaction* (Modern English Publications 1978)

HYMES, D 'On Communicative Competence' in GUMPERZ and HYMES (eds) (1970)

JOHNSON, K 'Adult Beginners: a Functional, or just a Communicative Approach' (Mimeo, and in revised form in *Modern English Teacher* 2/1978)

JOHNSON, K 'Communicative Approaches and Communicative Processes' in BRUMFIT and JOHNSON (1979)

JOHNSON, K 'Making Drills Communicative' (*Modern English Teacher*, 7/4 April 1980)

JOHNSON, K *Communicate in Writing* (Longman 1981)

JOHNSON, K 'Communicative Writing Practice and Aristotelian Rhetoric'. (In (ed) FREEDMAN, A, PRINGLE, I, YALDEN, J selected papers from the Carleton Conference on the Teaching of Writing, Longman forthcoming)

JOHNSON, K and MORROW, K E *Approaches* (Cambridge University Press 1979)

JUPP, T C and HODLIN'S *Industrial English* (Heinemann 1975)

KAMEEN, P T 'A Mechanical, Meaningful and Communicative Framework for ESL Sentence Combining Exercises' *(TESOL Quarterly*, 12, 4, 1978)

KERR, J Y K *Picture Cue Cards* (Evans 1979)

KERR, J Y K and LEISCHING, G (eds) *The Listening Library* (E.L.T. Materials: Design and Use No. 5, The British Council)

KRASHEN, S D 'The Monitor Model for Adult Second Language Performance'. (In BURT, DULAY, FINNOCARIO (eds), *Viewpoints on English as a Second Language* Regents 1977)

LEVINE, J 'Learning as they go' Paper delivered at the AILA/BAAL seminar on the Communicative Teaching of English, Lancaster 1973 (Mimeo)

LOZANOV, G *Suggestology and Outlines of Suggestopedy* (Gordon and Breach 1978)

LUNZER, E and GARDNER, K (eds) *The Effective use of Reading* (Heinemann 1979)

MALEY, A *Surrealistic English* (Cambridge University Press forthcoming)

MALEY, A and DUFF, A *Sounds Interesting* (Cambridge University Press, 1977)

MALEY, A and DUFF, A *Drama Techniques in Language Learning* (Cambridge University Press 1978)

MALEY, A and DUFF, A *Variations on a Theme* (Cambridge University Press 1979)

MALEY, A and DUFF, A *Sounds Intriguing* (Cambridge University Press 1979)

MALEY, A and GRELLET, A *Mind Matters* (Cambridge University Press forthcoming)

MOORWOOD, H (ed) *Selections from Modern English Teacher* (Longman 1978)

MORROW, K E *Skills for Reading* (Oxford University Press 1980)

MORROW, K E and JOHNSON, K *Communicate* (Cambridge University Press 1979)

MOULDING, S 'Developing all Four Skills' *(Modern English Teacher* 5/4, 1977)

MUNBY, J *Communicative Syllabus Design* (Cambridge University Press 1978)

NEWMARK, L 'How not to interfere with language learning' *(International Journal of American Linguistics* 32/1, 1966. Reprinted in BRUMFIT and JOHNSON (eds) (1979))

NEWMARK, L and REIBEL, D A 'Necessity and Sufficiency in Language Learning' *(International Review of Applied Linguistics* 6/2, 1968)

O'NEILL, T and SNOW, P *Crescent English Course* (Oxford University Press 1977)

PANSELOW, J and CRYMES, R H *On TESOL 76* (TESOL, Washington D.C. 1976)

PUGH, A K *Silent Reading: an Introduction to its Study and Teaching* (Heinemann 1978)

RAIMES, A 'A Grammar for Composition: the Grammar of Cohesion', Paper delivered at the TESOL Thirteenth Annual Convention, Boston, Mass., March 1979. (Mimeo)

RICHTERICH, R 'Definition of language needs and types of adults'. (Council of Europe, 1973)

RILEY, P and ZOPPIS, C 'The Sound and Video Library: an interim report on an experiment'. (Mélanges Pédagogiques (C.R.A.P.E.L. Nancy), 1976)

RIVERS, W *Teaching Foreign Language Skills* (University of Chicago Press 1966)

RIXON, S (ed) *Communication Games* (E.L.T. Materials: Design and Use No. 4, The British Council, 1974)

ROBINSON, F P *Effective Study* (Harper and Row 1946)

SCOTT, R and ARNOLD, J W *Starting Points* (Longman 1978)

STERN, H H 'Languages for younger children: recent trends and new directions'. Paper presented at the AILA/FIPLV Seminar, Feb. 1972 (Mimeo)

STERN, H H 'Optimal Age: Myth or Reality?' (*Canadian Modern Language Review* 32/3, 1976)

STEVICK, E *Memory, Meaning and Method* (Newbury House 1976)

STURTRIDGE, G and GEDDES, M *Reading Links*. (Heinemann forthcoming)

SUTHERLAND, J (ed) *The Oxford Book of English Talk* (Clarendon Press 1953)

TRIM, J L M 'Draft outline of a European Unit/Credit System for Modern Language Learning by Adults' (Council of Europe, 1973)

TRIM, J L M 'Report on some possible lines of development of an overall structure for a European Unit/Credit Scheme for foreign-language learning by adults' (Council of Europe 1977)

WHITE, R V 'Integrating Reading and Writing' (*Modern English Teacher* 6/3, 1978)

WHITE, R V *Functional English* (Nelson 1979)

WIDDOWSON, H G 'Two Types of Communication Exercise' in WIDDOWSON (1979)

WIDDOWSON, H G 'The Authenticity of Language Data' in PANSELOW and CRYMES (1976)

WIDDOWSON, H G *Teaching Language as Communication* (Oxford University Press 1978)

WIDDOWSON, H G *Explorations in Applied Linguistics* (Oxford University Press 1979)

WILKINS, D A 'An Investigation into the Linguistic and Situational Common Core in a Unit/Credit System' (Council of Europe 1973)

WILKINS, D A *Notional Syllabuses* (Oxford University Press 1976)

WRIGHT, A *Visual Materials for the Language Teacher* (Longman 1976)

WRIGHT, A and BETTERIDGE, D 'Writing a foreign language course: one project team's experience'. (E.L.T. Documents 76/2, The British Council 1976)